How To Books

Writing
Well at Work

Writing
Well at Work

*How to make an impact and
get results with your business
correspondence*

NICK VANDOME

How To Books

First published by How To Books Ltd, 3 Newtec Place,
Magdalen Road, Oxford OX4 1RE, United Kingdom.
Tel: (01865) 793806. Fax: (01865) 248780.
email: info@howtobooks.co.uk
www.howtobooks.co.uk

British Library Cataloguing in Publication Data
A catalogue record for this book is available from the
British Library

Editing by Alison Wilson
Cartoons by Mike Flanagan
Cover design by Shireen Nathoo Design
Cover image PhotoDisc

Produced for How To Books by Deer Park Productions.
Typeset by Anneset, Weston-super-Mare, Somerset.
Printed and bound by Cromwell Press, Trowbridge,
Wiltshire.

NOTE: The material contained in this book is set out in
good faith for general guidance and no liability can be
accepted for loss or expense incurred as a result of
relying in particular circumstances on statements made in
this book. The law and regulations may be complex and
liable to change, and readers should check the current
position with the relevant authorities before making
personal arrangements.

Contents

List of illustrations

Preface

Business writing may not have the same appeal as writing a romantic novel or a best-selling thriller, but is an area that touches more people than almost any other genre of writing. It is a skill that is easily picked up and refined and once you have mastered it then you will never look back.

Anyone who undertakes any business writing, whether it is a short letter or a complex report, can always improve their writing style and presentation skills. The business writer who thinks that he or she has nothing to learn is invariably the one who produces the most impenetrable documents. If someone is willing to take the time to practise the skills of business writing then they should soon see the rewards of their labour. This book is intended for anyone who wants to find out about the different areas of business writing, or brush up on the skills that they already have.

The rewards from good business writing accrue not only to the organisation in which they are produced: individuals can also benefit greatly from learning how to produce effective business documents. Initially, there is the advantage of feeling more confident in yourself – if you feel you are well equipped to do a job then you will approach it with greater enthusiasm and so be more likely to succeed. Also, as you become known as a reliable writer of business documents you will be entrusted with a greater number of tasks and also more important ones. More wide ranging benefits include the fact that business writing is a portable skill and one that may help you find a new or better job (which is always a consideration in today's unpredictable job market). Finally, you may also benefit in your activities outside the office: your personal business correspondence will be greatly improved and if you need to do tasks such as producing a newsletter for your local club then you will be able to impress your friends with your professional skills.

The way a business document looks is sometimes as important as what it says. Throughout this book, attention is given to style as well as substance. Numerous illustrations are included and, hopefully, these will provide readers with the knowledge to write and produce business documents that look professional and convey a clear and concise message.

Business writing need not be stuffy and boring: it can be as creative and satisfying as you want to make it. It can also be a valuable asset to your career – so get writing.

Nick Vandome

1

Defining Business Writing

Most people, even if they are not directly involved in business, have probably written some form of business communication. This may just be a letter to the bank manager asking for an overdraft, or a letter of complaint to a large organisation. Whatever the type of communication, it is fair to say that business writing touches us all at some point in our lives. It is therefore important to know what it is, how to do it, and how to do it effectively. For people who create business writing in their day-to-day jobs, it is a vital skill and one that is frequently overlooked.

OUTLINING THE AREAS OF BUSINESS WRITING

Business writing covers a lot more than just the occasional letter or report every once in a while. The genre encompasses a wide range of communications and styles and these can generally be divided into the following three categories:

1. Functional communication documents.
2. Presentational documents.
3. Information documents.

Communicating clearly

Although all business documents are about communication, to a greater or lesser extent, there are some where the message is the all-important aspect. This covers items such as letters, memos, reports and proposals. While all of these should be presented as professionally as possible, it is what is actually said that will be remembered. Because of this, functional documents should follow a few essential guidelines:

- **Clarity** is vital. If the message is confused or garbled then the purpose of the document will not be achieved.

- All documents should be as **concise** as possible. Points should be made as quickly and efficiently as possible: the world of business writing is inhibited by a lot of busy people who have no time for padding or waffle.

- Do not embellish your writing. It is a misconception that complicated words and long sentences make business writing more impressive. In fact, the opposite is true and sometimes **simplicity** is the key.

Making it look good

We live in an age where substance is frequently sacrificed in favour of style. In business writing the substance of a document is at least as important as the way it looks. However, this does not mean that business writing has to be dull and staid. In some cases the style is what leads the reader into the substance of the text. This is particularly true of items such as magazines, newsletters, press releases and promotional material. The aim here is to catch the reader's eye with the way the publication looks and then win them over with the message itself.

When you are considering the image of a business document keep a few points in mind:

- Who is the audience?

- What facilities do you have for producing the document?

- Do you have the ability to produce an attractive and eye-catching publication?

- Is there a budget for presentational material?

Producing business documents that look good and are effective is a skill that can be learned, but it is not something that can be picked up overnight. Careful thought and preparation should always go into the presentational side of business writing.

Sending and receiving information

The third type of business writing is concerned with **passing on** and **receiving** information and data, through forms, questionnaires and surveys. Although we may shudder at the mere thought of these types of documents, they are a vital part of the business world. Whether it is information for tax returns, market research or a staff opinion survey, businesses and individuals rely on data collected by these types of business writing.

The important thing to remember when creating forms, questionnaires and surveys is that they are useless if they are confusing for the user to fill in. You can create the most stylish questionnaire around but if people are intimidated or puzzled by it then they will not bother to complete it and so the whole point of the exercise will be wasted.

Points to consider
Before you start creating documents that will enable people to send back information you should ask yourself a few questions:

• Is too much information asked for in the document? (People get put off by book-like forms or questionnaires with hundreds of questions.)

• Are all of the questions clear and unambiguous? (If in doubt show it to a few colleagues to see what they think.)

• Is it easy for people to fill in and return? (This includes the use of check boxes, multiple choice questions and a prepaid reply envelope.)

A good way to test whether a form or a questionnaire is effective is to look at the quality of information that they provide. If this is inaccurate or incorrect then it is back to the drawing-board.

TARGETING YOUR AUDIENCE

Because of the wide range of people who receive business correspondence of one type or another, it can be one of the most challenging and exacting forms of writing. One day you may be writing an in-depth, complex proposal for the managing director and the next you may be writing a light-hearted feature for the office newsletter. Because of this it is important to identify your audience before you start writing. If you know exactly who is going to be reading your work then you can adapt your style accordingly.

Undertaking some research
Research is a vital part of any form of writing and this is certainly so in the world of business writing. But while research into the relevant topic can be rigorous and extensive, how often do people really look into who is going to be reading their words of wisdom? It is just as important to research your audience as it is to check the facts and figures for the document itself. For example:

• What is the age range of your audience?

- Will the document be seen externally as well as internally? If so you will have to be aware of the need to explain abbreviations and terms that are specific to your own organisation.

- Is your work going to be seen by someone who favours a particular style of writing?

Setting the tone

Once you have established who is going to be reading your work you can adapt your writing accordingly. In most cases this will mean aiming for a tone that is clear and approachable. Very few people like, or even understand, long, complicated sentences that are packed full of words plucked straight out of a thesaurus. Try not to be too verbose or pompous and always write for the people with the least amount of knowledge.

The one exception to this rule is business people who like to define themselves by how clever and educated they are. Unfortunately, there are a lot of these types around and most organisations have them. These are people who revel in jargon, legalese, convoluted sentences and impressive words (as they see them). They believe that because they can understand this overblown style of writing then it makes them better or more intelligent than their colleagues. Of course this is nonsense, but with people like this it is best to massage their egos and present them with the type of prose that they would write themselves. This is only a good idea if no one else is going to read the document and it should be remembered that this type of writing is for a very small audience (hopefully).

BENEFITING FROM GOOD BUSINESS WRITING

Achieving a professional image

As methods of presentation in the business world become ever more sophisticated, so more is expected in terms of style and professionalism. In many quarters it is no longer acceptable to hand in a dog-eared report or smudgy proposal. People are looking for slick and high quality documents and it is up to the person producing them to live up to these expectations. This applies equally to the way documents look and also the quality of the writing itself.

If you are thorough and conscientious in preparing and producing business documents then you will notice some immediate benefits:

- People will begin reading your documents in a positive frame of mind. First impressions are important and if your reader thinks that you have a good understanding of what you are doing then this gets things off to a favourable start.

- People will be able to save time if your documents are clearly written and well presented.

- Your organisation as a whole will benefit and this should reflect well on you.

- You may be asked to produce more and more documents and so become thought of as an expert in this area. It never does any harm to have a particular skill that is recognised throughout the organisation.

Increasing your confidence

Although business writing can be a little daunting at first it is actually one writing discipline that is relatively easy to learn. Once you understand the basics of what is required (being clear, concise and informative) it is possible to make great strides through practice and observation. This means writing as much as you can yourself and also reading widely in the area of business writing so that you can identify what is good, bad or indifferent and so act accordingly.

The more business writing that you do then the better you will become at it. This will not happen overnight but if you try and produce business documents on a regular basis then your style and presentation will improve. With this improvement should come greater **self-confidence**, as you realise that business writing is not as difficult as you first feared and that you are actually quite good at it. This confidence will then transfer itself to your writing, leading to even more impressive results. And if you think that you are doing a good job then this may very well reflect in other duties in the workplace. Overall, good business writing is something that can bring tangible benefits to both the individual and the organisation.

TACKLING PROOF-READING

One area of business writing that is sometimes overlooked is proof-reading the finished document. In general this is a tedious task that no one likes doing and it is usually a prime candidate for ending up in the 'pending' tray. However, it should be looked at as an integral part of the writing process and be given as much attention as any other area. There are two main types of proof-reading:

1. Proof-reading your own original work to check for accuracy and clarity.

2. Proof-reading a draft version and the final version of someone else's work. This involves comparing two versions of the same document and it is essential that you do not get the two mixed up.

Being a thorough proof-reader

Good proof-reading is a lot more than just checking for typing errors and incorrectly spelt words. It is also about checking and refining your writing so that your final version is as polished and professional as possible. A good proof-reader will have to take into consideration everything from passive writing to the use of Plain English.

Tautology

This is essentially saying the same thing twice and therefore using redundant words, *eg* 'a round circle' or 'came one after another in succession'. Tautology usually occurs when the writer has an important point to make and tries to achieve this by repetition. This is unnecessary and only serves to make a sentence appear cumbersome. This is certainly a case when the maxim of 'less is more' can be applied.

Duplicated words

This usually occurs through typing error or because a word is repeated at the end of one line and then at the beginning of the next one. Spell checkers can pick this up but it is something that should be watched for carefully when you are proof-reading your final copy.

Passive voice

Writing in the passive voice is often associated with writing that is impersonal and laborious. **Active writing** conveys a more upbeat image and usually contributes to shorter, sharper sentences.

Passive writing occurs when the verb and the agent (the performer of the action) of a sentence are different, *eg* 'The road was crossed by the chicken'. In this example the subject is the road and the agent is the chicken, thus giving a passive sentence because the subject and the agent are different. To make this sentence active it would become, 'The chicken crossed the road'. Here the chicken is both the subject and the agent and so the sentence is active. Passive sentences are easy to recognise because they almost always have part of the verb 'to be' (is, have been, was, were, have been) and a past participle (crossed, chosen, written). Some word processing packages have grammar checkers that are able to identify passive writing – but beware of some of the alternatives that they suggest.

Spelling
If proof-reading is done conscientiously then there is no real excuse for incorrectly spelt words in the final document. There is a simple way to ensure that any words you are unsure about are correct: look them up in the dictionary. This may sound like the ultimate in commonsense but it is amazing how often people cannot be bothered using a dictionary, or do not feel it is necessary, because they 'think' that a word is spelt correctly. If you know you have problems with certain words (everyone has their own blank spots when it comes to spelling, whether it is 'accommodate', necessary' or 'presence') then make a point of looking them up until you are sure that you have mastered them. Spell checkers on computers are useful up to a point, but they will not pick up words that are spelt correctly as another word, *eg* 'presents' instead of 'presence'.

Plain English
The essence of Plain English is to make the written word as clear as possible. This applies doubly so in business writing, where people sometimes have a tendency to use long words and sentences because they think it will impress their colleagues. In fact the opposite is true: pretentious or overblown writing impresses few people, particularly if it does not make sense. If possible, replace long or difficult words with shorter, simpler ones (*eg* 'talkative' instead of 'loquacious', or 'help' instead of 'facilitate') and keep your sentences and paragraphs to a reasonable length. This does not mean you have to reduce your writing to the level of a Janet and John book; just bear in mind that no one is going to be impressed by something that they cannot understand.

- For further information about the concept of Plain English contact: Campaign for Plain English, PO Box 3, New Mills, High Peak SK22 4QP. Tel: (01633) 744409.

Biased writing
In this age of political correctness you should keep an eye out for biased writing, that directly or indirectly offends a group in society. This includes remarks that could cause offence on the grounds of gender, race, religion, age or physical appearance. Try to avoid stereotypes, such as referring to all pilots as 'he' and all cabin crew as 'she',

and always be especially careful when referring to ethnic and religious groups.

Breaking the rules
English grammar is festooned with rules and regulations, some of them dating back hundreds of years. But trends change and this even applies to the archaic world of grammar. It is now generally accepted that it is perfectly feasible to start sentences with words such as 'And', 'But' and 'Because', or to end sentences with a preposition and even to split infinitives, if the mood takes you. Of course some rules of grammar are there for good reasons, but others have been followed more out of habit than anything else. A good rule of thumb is that if something makes sense and reads well then it should be left well alone.

There are several good books that cover the basics of English grammar and three of them are:

1. *Collins Gem English Grammar*, Ronald G. Hardie, HarperCollins.

2. *English Grammar, An Outline*, Rodney Huddleston, Cambridge University Press.

3. *Teach Yourself English Grammar*, B. Phythian, Hodder & Stoughton.

Page numbers and chapter headings
One area of proof-reading that is sometimes overlooked is that of page numbers and chapter headings. These should always be checked carefully to make sure that they correspond to the correct part of the document. If there is a list of contents, this should also be checked to make sure that the headings correspond exactly to the actual headings in the document. This can be done as a separate part of the proof-reading process, once the text itself has been checked.

THE PRACTICALITIES OF PROOF-READING

Making time for proofing
Although proof-reading may seem like a simple, if tedious, task, it is not. It is a writing skill just like any other and one that needs high levels of concentration and accuracy. It is not something that you can skim through and hope for the best. Because of this, it is a good idea to set aside a specific time of the day if you know you have proof-reading to do. This way you will increase the chances of it actually being done, rather than put off indefinitely.

Since proof reading requires a lot of concentration it is best not to do too much in one session. Half an hour at a time is a reasonable maximum and certainly no more than an hour. Take regular breaks, if only to rest your eyes; do not worry if you have to leave something and go back to it. Try to eliminate distractions by telling your colleagues that you are proof-reading or put a little sign on the top of your computer. There is nothing worse than being interrupted when you have your mind focused on proof-reading.

Using hard copy
Most people like writing on computer screens, but hate reading on them. This is generally because of the slight glare that they give off and also because you have to scroll down the screen to read the entire document. When you are proof-reading it is strongly recommended that you print off a hard copy of the document before you start. This will not only spare you a headache later in the day; it will also improve your proof-reading accuracy.

In the future it may be easier to undertake proof-reading on screen because computer monitors are being developed to give the appearance of reading ink on paper. However, it will be several years before these are adopted as the norm in the business world.

Proof-reading in pairs
The best way to check a document is to have one person reading the original out loud and another one comparing a copy for accuracy. However, this is not always possible and it cannot be done if you are checking your own original document. In cases like this it is a good idea to give it to someone else to proof-read: sometimes you become so familiar with your own writing that you are unaware of even the most obvious mistakes. A fresh perspective can work wonders in cases like this.

SUMMARY

1. You do not have to have a complicated and pompous style to be a good business writer. The best type of business writing is clear and informative.

2. It is important to know the audience, since business writing covers a huge range of people and groups. It is vital to know who you are addressing as this will have a significant impact on the tone of your document.

3. Careful proof-reading is essential in business writing. Documents that have not been proof-read properly will appear sloppy and convey an unprofessional image, which is the last thing you want in business.

ACTION POINTS

1. Make a list of all of the people you send business correspondence to. Ask yourself if you would address them in the same way and with the same tone.

2. Make a list of all the different types of business correspondence that you do. Analyse how you approach and produce each of these.
3. Buy a good book about English grammar and make sure that you read it and understand it.

4. Compile a procedure for proof-reading, *ie* methods for checking spelling, grammar, typos *etc*.

5. Learn the professional marks for proof-reading. This will remove any ambiguity and show that you are serious about what you do.

2

Producing Effective Reports

Perhaps it is a hangover from schooldays, but whenever the word 'report' is mentioned in the workplace most employees run for cover. The idea of researching, writing and presenting a report on almost any topic is a daunting prospect for most people and one that is unlikely to produce many willing volunteers. Despite this, reports and report writing are an integral part of the business world and sooner or later you may be asked, or told, to put together an effective report.

Business reports come in many shapes and sizes and can include a wide variety of topics. Some of these are:

- research reports
- health and safety reports
- industrial relations reports
- evaluation reports
- system reports
- staff appraisal reports
- competitive tendering reports
- feasibility reports.

All of the above have their own specific purpose and for the novice report writer it can be perplexing just trying to work out how to start. But with the correct planning the whole project can be made to look a whole lot easier.

Planning your report

The first step is to identify the tasks that you will have to undertake. These fall into four categories:

1. Finding out what is expected of you and your report.
2. Researching the topic and learning as much about it as possible.
3. Writing the report.
4. Presenting the finished article.

FOLLOWING YOUR BRIEF

Obtaining a brief

Preparation and planning are the keys to a professional and effective report. This obviously applies to the report writer and it should also apply to the person who has commissioned the report. However, the person doing the commissioning is not always as well prepared as they should be. They may approach you with a vague request to 'produce a report on the increased levels of production in the widget section'. With this flimsy instruction you will be expected to produce an accurate and concise report. Unfortunately, without more information about what is wanted this is just not possible – you do not know the intended audience, the purpose of the report, its length or how it is going to be used. At this point you have to take the bull by the horns and ask for a specific brief for the report.

A **brief** is a set of instructions that should provide an outline for the final report. Without one it is like trying to build a house without any plans or drawings. The brief should include information such as:

- The length of the report.
- Who is going to be reading it?
- The aim of the report – *ie* what is it intended to achieve.
- The timescale for producing the report.

Although you may feel uneasy about doing so, you should discuss the brief in as much detail as possible with the person who has asked you to write the report. It is important that you are absolutely clear about what is expected of you and that you are confident about the brief. If any points need to be clarified say so at the outset because it will save a great deal of embarrassment and anguish later on.

Creating an outline from the brief

Once the brief has been agreed an **outline** of the report can be created. This is the skeleton on which you are going to hang the flesh and blood of the finished document. The outline has to provide you with a working document, which you can then develop and amend as you go along. If nothing else, it gives you a chance to get your initial ideas down on paper. You could create the outline in a variety of formats:

- rough, hand-written notes

- a synopsis of all of the major points that need to be covered

- a structured list, detailing each section of the report in turn

- the headings and sub-headings that you intend to use in the report itself.

However you structure your outline it is important that you take the time and effort to do it properly. If you rush through it, in your eagerness to get to the report proper, then this will catch up with you and you may find yourself stumbling halfway through lack of preparation. A well thought-out and structured outline should serve the following purposes:

1. Clearly state the purpose of the report and who it is for.

2. Set out the main arguments and themes of the report.

3. Establish the style in which the report will be written (following a house style or a new approach).

4. Identify the various sections of the report, from the title page to the index.

A good outline will ensure that the writing of the report itself is a much less painful task than maybe was first imagined. Indeed, it may even seem as if the words are falling into place by themselves. If this is the case it will be through hard work rather than any form of luck. A professional and well-structured outline is one that can be handed over to a colleague and they are then able to write the report from it. This is the real test of an outline and it is worth trying.

GATHERING INFORMATION

Information that you already have

Finding the facts to put in a report is not an optional task. Without facts your report will just be a loose collection of your own ideas and theories. This is not a report, it is an essay. A report needs hard facts, not only for their own sake but also to support arguments and premises. Much of this type of information should already be available within your own organisation. A good starting point is to write a list, itemising the general areas from where you might need to get information. The following sections could then cover these:

- finance
- personnel

- marketing
- sales
- communications.

Do not be afraid to approach people in different parts of the organ-isation for information but make sure you let them know what it is for. If you are secretive it will only make people think that you are up to something suspicious. Another good source of information is your company's Annual Report. This will not only provide you with general and financial information but it may also give you some ideas about how to present a report.

Researching new information

At some stage during the creation of your report you will realise that not all of the information you need is held within your own office. This may be at the outline writing stage, or it may be when you are halfway through the report itself. The information you need could be a particular statistic, a quote, or a paper that was written ten years earlier. Even though at the time this may seem like a major hurdle there is no need to panic. There are numerous resources available from which a variety of data can be obtained.

The Internet

Perhaps the most widely publicised and promoted communications and research device of the 1990s, the Internet has information on every subject you could imagine, and many more besides. Basically it is a collection of millions of pages of information, held on comput-ers around the world that are connected electronically so that they can be viewed on any compatible computer. The system itself is the Internet while the pages of information are known as the **World Wide Web** (WWW). To gain access to the WWW you need a computer (a PC or an Apple Mac are the most common), a web browser (free software that acts as a window to the Internet), a modem and an Internet Service Provider (ISP). ISPs are companies who physically manage the link between you and the Internet. Most of them charge for this service but it is usually only in the region of £10 per month. On top of this you will be charged at the cost of a local phone call for the time you are connected to the Internet. The resources on the Internet border on the endless, ranging from databases of major libraries to home-made pages created by amateur enthusiasts. If you cannot find the information you are looking for on the Internet then it probably does not exist. But a word of warning: in addition to the useful data on the Internet there is an awful lot of junk. This sometimes means that searching the Internet is a tedious process and it is with good reason that some people have nicknamed it the World Wide Wait. However, as technology improves so should the response times and it is one research tool that is definitely worth checking out.

Libraries

Perhaps these are now regarded as a little old-fashioned when compared with the technological wizardry of the information superhighway. However, nothing could be further from the truth and libraries are still an excellent source of facts and figures. Their great advantage is the human factor: if the information is not available then the librarian will probably know where it can be obtained.

Relevant associations

Virtually every organisation or body of people, whether it is nuclear scientists or flower arrangers, has a relevant association. These are a valuable source of research since they will have not only a wealth of information at their disposal, but also a number of useful contacts. If you approach them openly then they will probably be only too pleased to help.

Public bodies

Government and council offices can be a goldmine as far as gathering official information is concerned. They are particularly useful for providing facts and figures, such as regional unemployment figures or the levels of house sales across the country, and they are becoming increasingly aware that they can provide a valuable service. This means that you are more likely to get the information that you want but it also means that you might have to pay for it.

Newspapers

These remain another invaluable source of information but you should not restrict yourself to your own daily paper. Most broadsheet newspapers operate their own press cuttings service that they will be only too willing to share with you, for a price. Also, our friend the Internet has on-line versions of newspapers from around the world so you will be able to scan the *San Francisco Chronicle* or the *Melbourne Age* for any snippets of information that may be of use to you.

STRUCTURING AN EFFECTIVE REPORT

Unlike some other forms of business writing, the structure of a report is fairly rigid and there is not much room for manoeuvre. This is a good thing if you like to have a clear idea of what you are doing but it may be a disadvantage if you consider yourself a bit of a literary free-spirit. People who are slightly daunted about structuring a report only have to go back to school essays and remember the idea of a beginning, a middle and an end. This is the simple part. The real trick is knowing what to put into each section.

Setting out the beginning

The beginning of a report is not something that needs passages of purple prose to catch the reader's attention. Unfortunately it is a lot more prosaic than that. It should contain certain items of factual information that will help ease the reader into the report so that they know exactly what to expect. These should include:

- A **title page**. This consists of the name of the report, its subject matter, the author(s), their position in the organisation and the date of publication (see Figure 1).

- A **contents list**. This is a precise list of what is in the report. It should list all of the relevant sections and sub-sections. Page numbers should also be included (see Figure 2).

- An **introduction**. A few paragraphs that tell the reader the subject of the report, why it has been written and any acknowledgements that are required.

- A **summary**. This is a general overview of the contents of the report. It should give the reader a good idea about what is in the full report.

The beginning of the report could also include a foreword or a preface, written by someone not directly connected with the report but who is acknowledged as an expert or an authority in their own field. However, this is not a common device to use in report writing and in general the information in the beginning of a report should be concise and specific.

Producing the middle

The middle part of any report is the real meat of the document. This is where the purpose of the report will be detailed and the arguments will be made. A number of issues can be considered when dealing with the main part of the report:

- The structure of the report should be logical and ordered. This is not the time to start exercising your literacy pretensions.

- Begin by setting out the reasons for writing the report.

- Make sure that facts and figures are included to support any claims that are made.

- Use a separate paragraph for each new idea or argument.

- Keep the language clear and explain all instances of jargon and acronyms.

The length of the middle of the report is entirely dependent on the subject matter and the arguments that are being put forward. Some reports are only half a dozen pages in length while others can be ten or 20 times that length. When writing the report it is best not to worry too much about the length of it. Write what you think needs to be included and do not try and pad it out or edit it unnecessarily. There is no regulation for the length of a report so go with your intuition and write it to a length with which you feel comfortable.

Finishing at the end

Conclusions
The main item that comes at the end of the report is the conclusion and this is a vital part of the document. This is where you draw together all of the ideas and arguments that have been made in the body of the report. The conclusion is likely to be the last thing that the readers will read and it needs to be powerful and persuasive to ensure that it makes a lasting impact. Before the report is written you will have a rough idea of the recommendations that you want to make in the conclusion. If these are kept in mind during the writing of the report then the conclusion will follow seamlessly on from the main report.

Before you start writing the conclusion it is a good idea to read through the whole report and take notes as you go. This may seem like doing the same work twice but it can be easy to lose sight of the

The effectiveness of the single flange widget

A report into the development and marketing possibilities of the flanget

By   Andrew Cotton, Chief Development Officer
      Steve Bryson, Senior Technician, New Products
      Sarah Hartson, Sales Executive, New Products

Contact: Andrew Cotton, extension 32998

17 October 1999

Fig. 1. Sample report covers.

The effectiveness of the single flange widget

A report into the development and
marketing possibilities of the flanget

By   Andrew Cotton, Chief Development Officer
Steve Bryson, Senior Technician, New Products
Sarah Hartson, Sales Executive, New Products

Contact:
Andrew Cotton

17 October 1999

Fig. 1. continued.

Contents

Fig. 2. The contents page of a report.

message that you want to convey. These notes can then be used as an outline for the conclusion. Make sure that you summarise all of the main points and ideas in the report and draw logical and precise conclusions from these. Do not waffle and never introduce new information that has not previously been dealt with (it is not a thriller you are writing, where you can introduce a new character in the last chapter to explain miraculously who the murderer is). Nothing in the conclusion should be a surprise or a shock. Some features to look out for are:

- Recommendations based on what has been stated in the report. Do not make these exaggerated or extreme – sometimes the simplest suggestion is the best one.

- Further study. You may conclude that the subject of your report needs further research and examination. If so, state this and give your reasons.

- No action required. We do not always realise the value of what we already have in front of us and sometimes it takes a detailed look at something to reveal its true worth.

Additional end matter
As well as the conclusion, the end of a report will also include all or some of the following:

- A **glossary**. This is a list of words or phrases that may need to be explained to the reader. If this is an extensive list then it is a good idea to look through the text of the report to see how well these terms have been described originally. It is not a good idea to make the reader constantly look up a glossary to make sense of what has been written.

- A **bibliography**. This is an index of all the relevant reference material that has been used for the report. State the title of the publication, the author, the publisher, the edition and the date of publication.

- An **index**. As with a standard index in any non-fiction book, this will include all of the relevant topics and names in the report. They should be listed with the page number(s) on which they appear.

GETTING YOUR MESSAGE ACROSS

Defining an effective writing style

No one would ever claim that report writing is the pinnacle of literacy achievement. Reports are not renowned for their sparkling style or linguistic artistry. In fact the writing style of reports can quite justifiably be described as strait-laced, and with good reason. More than almost any other type of document a report needs to put forward the information it contains in the clearest and most straightforward way. If the prose detracts from what is being said in the report then the writer is not doing his or her job properly.

However, this is not to say that it is easy to produce the right tone for report writing. If you try and be too serious and solemn then the reader will become bored alarmingly quickly. If you try and add too much zest into the prose then the reader may pay more attention to the style than to the substance. Like every other form of writing, getting the right tone for reports requires practice. If you are new to report writing try the following two exercises:

1. Get your hands on half a dozen reports. Read through them and then list them in order, best to worst, as far as effectiveness is concerned. To judge this, look at whether they held your interest and how good they were at getting their points across. Once you have done this, go back through the reports and analyse what you consider to be good and bad in each one. This way you will be able to build up a reference point for your own report writing style. The things that you should be looking for are: word usage; sentence length, paragraph length; clarity of arguments; and the effectiveness of the overall structure.

2. Try writing some short sample reports, using a variety of styles. Give them to colleagues and ask them to summarise what the reports are about. If they are able to do this accurately and easily then there is a good chance that you have discovered a reasonable writing style for reports.

Achieving a readable report writing style will take time and a reasonable amount of practice. But it is worth persevering with, because it is a valuable talent to develop and you will find you are much in demand once you have done so.

HOLDING ATTENTION

Making it look good

Even though reports frequently cover serious and, at times, staid subject matter, this does not mean that you should not try and make them look as attractive and as professional as possible. If the document looks good then the initial impression will be favourable and the reader will begin the report in a positive frame of mind.

Formatting a report

Since a report is a serious factual document it does not have to be produced in a style that jumps off the page and makes the reader stand back in amazement. In fact the more unobtrusive the visual style is the better, as it will give the reader more of a chance to concentrate on the content. However, this is not to say that the style can be ignored: sometimes a great deal of thought has to go into making a document look simple but professional. Although the format of a report will not be as complicated as for a document such as a newsletter, a few areas still need careful consideration:

- **Choice of typeface.** The typeface for a report should be simple and uncomplicated. It can be either serif (with loops on the ends of the letters) or sans serif (without loops) but the one criterion is that it must not be gimmicky or distracting. As a rule, serif type creates a more traditional image while sans serif should be used if a more modern feel is required.

- **Size of typeface.** The size of the typeface (point size) should be big enough to read comfortably but not so big that it looks like a children's book. A point size of between 10 to 12 is usually acceptable, depending on how large this makes the chosen typeface look. Experiment to see what works best and always make your final choice from a hard copy rather than what you see on your computer screen.

- **Line spacing.** Although a report does not have to be double-spaced there should be at least one clear line between paragraphs and two between different sections. If possible, it is preferable to start each section on a new page. Make sure that each page of text does not look crushed and that there is plenty of white space to break up the text. This includes allowing generous margins on each page – one inch on all sides should be a minimum.

- **Page and paragraph numbering**. Each page of the report should be numbered, as should each paragraph. This makes it easy to find and refer to particular parts of the report.

Figure 3 shows an example of the style for a well-laid out report.

---

4. The current situation

Currently the market for widgets is thriving. A combination of strong overseas demand and a weak pound have contributed to ideal widget trading conditions. The outlook for the immediate future looks good and it is therefore vital that we are prepared for the challenges that lie ahead.

4.1 Production capacity

At present two Midlands factories are working at 95% of their optimum capacity and our Newcastle operation is only slightly behind at 92%. While both of these figures are excellent we need to be as flexible as possible in terms of meeting increased demand. If there is a sudden surge in demand, as is likely if trading conditions remain the same, then we may have to increase the capacity at all three factories to 97%.

4.2 Current demand

The current demand is strongest in our European sector, while global demand has only fallen marginally in the last three months. This suggests that the market is still relatively buoyant and seems likely to remain so.

4.2.1. Local demand

This is very encouraging in the north and east sectors, but the south and west sectors have experienced a slight dip. This could be because of a number of factors, including seasonal variations and poor weather over the summer months.

Fig. 3. A sample page for a report.

SUMMARY

1. You need to have a clear and precise brief for your report. If you do not have one then keep asking until you get one that you are completely happy with.

2. It is not important to be an expert on the topic about which you are writing the report. However, if there are areas in which your knowledge is lacking it is essential that you make the effort to fill in the gaps. Meticulous research is the best way to give yourself the knowledge and the confidence to produce an effective report.

3. Develop your own style for report writing. This should be a 'middle way' between dull, staid writing and extravagant 'purple' prose. In some cases it may be necessary to adapt your style of writing accordingly.

ACTION POINTS

1. Find as many research outlets as possible.

2. Get connected to the Internet. Check out different Internet Service Providers (ISPs) to find out which one offers the best package in terms of cost, service and response time on the Internet.

3. Read as many reports by other people as you can.

4. Polish your report writing style through practice. Do not just jump in at the deep end.

5. Ask colleagues for their opinions about your report and listen to their advice.

3

Creating Proposals That Work

Proposals occur regularly in business writing and they are a useful device for anyone who wants to promote their ideas and get themselves noticed. A good proposal can show that they are forward thinking and innovative and that you can also put your ideas across in a positive, professional manner. However, a poorly thought-out or presented proposal will immediately detract from the original idea, no matter how good it is. Proposals can be written for a variety of reasons and these include:

- Changing procedures.
- Introducing new systems or ways of working.
- Developing new projects and initiatives.
- Improving productivity and efficiency.

Together, a good idea and an effective proposal can have important implications for an organisation and also for the author of the proposal. In order to achieve this the proposal should be well thought-out, positive, persuasive and accurate.

ORDERING YOUR IDEAS

Brainstorming

Getting your ideas down
Before you even consider starting to write your proposal you will need to get your ideas onto paper. The importance of this is to give some structure to your document. Frequently when you are fired up with enthusiasm about a new idea it is easy to get carried away and spill all of your thoughts onto paper at once. Invariably, if you do this, your ideas will not appear in the same dynamic way that you imagined them in your head. For this reason you should sit down and get your ideas into some kind of order and structure.

Brainstorming consists of writing down the title of your proposal and then all the related topics you can think of. At this stage it does not matter how far-fetched or fanciful an idea may seem; this is a time for free association and what initially may seem like a crazy concept may, eventually, become an important part of the proposal. Brainstorming is all about getting ideas down on paper and getting your mind working. The keys to a good brainstorming session are:

- being imaginative

- being innovative

- thinking of the unconventional

- producing numerous ideas (if you write down ten headings and only use one then this is still a successful piece of brainstorming).

Although you can do brainstorming on your own, it does not have to be a solitary occupation: it can be an entertaining and productive exercise to do some brainstorming with other people. If you do this then you should remain receptive to everyone else's ideas and not feel self-conscious about your own. Do not be afraid of saying something that the others may think is daft – that is what brainstorming sessions are all about, so let your imagination run riot.

Creating a brainstorming chart
Once the ideas start flowing you will need to commit them to paper in some form. The best way to do this is on a sheet of paper (computers are not the best medium for conducting brainstorming sessions) with the title of your project written in the middle. For each idea, draw a line from the centre and write down a subheading. Continue doing this and then repeat for the next level. Eventually you will have something that looks like a mutant spider or octopus (see Figure 4).

Editing your brainstorming session
The first thing to do after a brainstorming session is to put your chart away in a drawer and leave it there for a couple of days. Then, when you look at it again you will be able to evaluate the content with a clear mind. This is vital when you are trying to separate the wheat from the chaff; if you try and edit your brainstorming too soon after the event then the ideas may still be too fresh in your mind and you will not be able to look at it objectively.

Do not be afraid to edit your ideas ruthlessly. The very nature of brainstorming means that a lot of what is produced will be unsuitable, irrelevant or just plain daft. Look at each item and ask yourself the following questions:

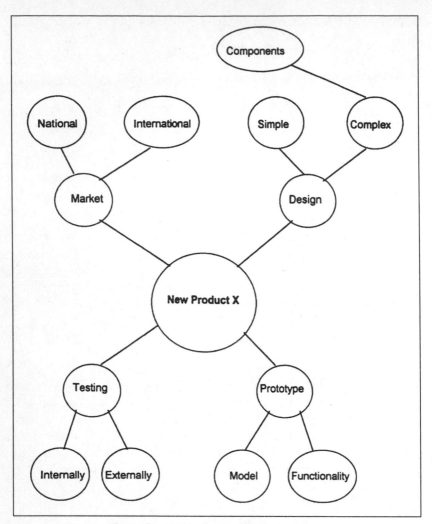

Fig. 4. Example of a brainstorming chart.

- Will this add something to the proposal?
- Is this the best way of conveying the theme of the proposal?
- Is this topic relevant and precise?

If the answers to these questions are yes, then you can include the topic in the proposal. If not, take a red pen and score it off. If you end up using ten per cent of the original brainstorming session then you are doing well. If you feel you do not have enough information then take what you have and go back to the brainstorming drawing-board.

LAYING OUT YOUR ARGUMENT

Creating a structured outline

Once you have taken your initial idea and subjected it to a brainstorming session, it is time to put down a structure for your proposal. As with many forms of writing this consists of the traditional beginning, middle and end, or 'Tell people what you are going to tell them, tell them, and then tell them what you have told them'. This may seem obvious but creating a logical structure that takes the reader through every step of the proposal and then presents them with a persuasive conclusion is vital to the success of your project.

Starting at the beginning

Since you will have probably been working on your proposal for a considerable amount of time it is easy to lose sight of the basics. But these need to be included right at the beginning of your proposal, as an introduction, no matter how obvious you feel they are. The people reading your proposal will have a variety of other reports and proposals to read so they will not want to waste time trying to work out what yours is all about. The areas you should cover in the introduction include:

- Exactly what your proposal is about.

- How you intend to implement your idea.

- The business benefits it is going to bring.

- How much it is going to cost.

- The short and long-term impact it is going to have on your organisation.

Each of these points should be put clearly and concisely – this is not a time for going into specific details. Emphasise the benefits but do not make any exaggerated claims that you will not be able to back up.

At the end of the introduction, include the names of the people who were involved in the proposal and a contact telephone number.

Preparing the middle

The middle, or body, of your proposal is the main part of your document. In it you will be giving a detailed account of the ground covered in the introduction. Each element needs to be explained with clarity and attention to detail. This is the part of the proposal on which your idea will stand or fall. When writing the middle of the proposal you should consider two particular areas.

1. Make sure you pay enough attention to describing what the proposal actually *is*. You will be very familiar with the project and you will know it inside out. However, the people reading your proposal will not be so informed about it so you will have to spell things out for them. Imagine that you do not know anything about the project and write from that viewpoint.

2. This is your main sales pitch so use it to promote your idea. Do not make exaggerated claims, but do not be afraid to stress the benefits of the proposal. Do not sell yourself short.

Finishing at the end
The end of the proposal should be a brief summary of what has gone before. This can be in the form of a couple of paragraphs or a list of bullet points. Include each of the main points in your proposal and also list the benefits of your project, keeping the most persuasive ones to the end so it is the last thing the reader sees. This should serve as a reminder rather than an opportunity to add new information. Also repeat the names of the authors of the proposal and the contact telephone number.

WRITING WITH CONFIDENCE

Achieving a positive style
If you have enough confidence in your project to present it to senior management then you should try and convey this confidence in your writing style. Since you will be dealing with busy people you do not want to produce a long-winded, turgid proposal that they have difficulty even finishing. You want to write something that is punchy, fast-paced, and catches the reader's imagination. To achieve this you should consider the following:

- Use **short sentences** and paragraphs. This injects a feeling of pace into writing and makes it easier for the reader to digest each point. This is a device employed by many thriller writers, particularly at moments of tension or excitement.

- **Avoid jargon** and technical terms. If you have to use them, then explain them at the outset, *eg* 'National Aeronautics and Space Administration (NASA)' or 'The company's multi-functional relaxation system – a bed'. Never presume that people will understand jargon, even if you think it is crystal clear.

- Use **bulleted** or **numbered lists**. These are excellent devices for presenting important or complicated pieces of information and they provide a good visual contrast to large areas of plain text.

- Use **one paragraph for each point** that you want to make. Do not combine separate ideas. This just creates confusion and gives the impression that you are not completely sure of your project.

Choosing your words

The words that you use in your proposal can be just as important as your writing style. As a general rule, use **short, simple words** rather than long ones. Avoid negative sounding words and try and substitute them with positive ones. Always try and convey a dynamic, positive impression. For instance, say, 'We will complete the project on time' rather than, 'We might complete the project on time, all things being well'. Words you should be using could include:

- positive
- succeed
- achieve
- accomplish
- triumph
- direct
- clear
- certainty
- save
- win
- deliver
- definite.

Try to avoid words such as the following:

- unfortunately
- defeat
- failure
- perhaps
- maybe
- collapse
- ruin
- deficient.

Always look at your chosen words carefully to make sure that they convey exactly what you want them to and that they could not be misconstrued in any way.

USING QUOTES AND EXAMPLES

Using quotes
Quotes and examples are vital to the success of any proposal. They put flesh on the bones of your arguments and add conviction to the points you are trying to make. If possible, you should always try and obtain quotes and examples that support the main points in your proposal.

Selecting quotes
Owing to the fact that quotes are a bit like statistics (there is always a quote or a statistic that can be produced to support the counter-argument) it is acceptable to find the quotes or examples that suit your own purposes. After all, you are trying to sell your proposal so it is perfectly legitimate to be selective in your use of quotes. If some-one else wants to dispute your point of view then it is up to them to find quotes and examples to support their own argument. However, this does not mean that you should be too selective when you are editing quotes. For instance, your quote may appear as, 'The findings of the committee concluded that . . . this project has the potential for enormous success'. This appears very positive, but if the section you have missed out reads, 'with a complete rethink and the investment of million of pounds', then it would put a very different slant on the quote. In general it is better to include complete quotes rather than edited ones so as to remove any doubt about them having been 'doctored'. And *never* make up quotes to suit your argument – it is unnecessary and if you are found out it will torpedo your whole project.

Gaining permissions
If you are using quotes of a few sentences in your proposal then you do not have to worry about contacting the source for permission to use the quote. (You should, however, always credit the source in your proposal – see Figure 5 for an example of incorporating a quote.) However, if you are using a longer quote, over 300 words, then you should think about asking for permission for its use. In practice this rarely happens for internal documents, as they are not usually pub-lished for a wider audience. But if you think the proposal may be

Some Internet users feel that the medium has got a little out of control and should be reined in by governments and interested parties. However, it is clear that not everyone is in favour of this pro-active regulatory approach:

Having worked with computers for more than twenty years it is my firmly held belief that the sprawling nature of the Internet is not only one of its great strengths; it is also vital to its survival. It is a living, evolving entity and any attempts to restrict this will result in the loss of its oxygen of innovation and without that it is nothing.

Simon Webster, *Computers Worldwide*
18 September 1999

Whether this happens remains to be seen, but it demonstrates the fact that some communications media rely heavily on the format that brought them into being in the first place.

Fig. 5. How to incorporate a quote.

published externally then it is worth keeping this in mind. One way around this is to keep your quotes and examples short and to the point – which is better for the style of your proposal in any case.

Finding quotes

Existing quotes
The most obvious way to get quotes and examples to support your proposal is to use ones already in magazines or publications. These can be found in a number of sources.

* **Trade magazines**. Some of these will probably be available in your own office and they should cover the general area that your proposal is about.

* **General interest magazines**. Business issues appear frequently in a variety of magazines from *Reader's Digest* to *Cosmopolitan* and so it is always worth keeping an eye out for them. This may depend on good luck rather than in-depth research but it can be a useful source.

* **Business sections** in newspapers. All broadsheet newspapers have extensive business reporting and features, which cover the whole

spectrum of the business world. The *Financial Times* is particularly useful in this respect.

- **The Internet**. Despite its occasional deficiencies, the Internet comes into its own when you are searching for a specific topic. For instance, if your proposal is about water-cooled nuclear reactors then all you have to do is type in the relevant words into one of the search engines (a device that searches through the pages on the World Wide Web to find the specified items) and then wait for a response. The search will probably show up hundreds of related items, including a lot of articles and quotes about your chosen subject.

If you have any problem in locating quotes from the above sources then try asking at your local library. Librarians are not only very helpful people but also experts at finding obscure pieces of information. In most cases they will be only too delighted to help you find a relevant quote for your project.

New quotes
Another way to obtain quotes for your proposal is to get original ones – straight from the horse's mouth. This can be done by contacting people who work in the area dealt with by your proposal, either by letter or telephone. You should not feel you are imposing on anyone, because most people enjoy talking about their specialist subject and if they do not then they will tell you so.

When you approach people for quotes you should try and find out something about their views on the subject that you want to discuss and also phrase your questions carefully. Ideally, you want them to say something that supports your argument but you should not put words into their mouth or try and twist the meaning of what they say.

GETTING YOUR PROPOSAL ACCEPTED

Concentrating on presentation
Having researched and written your proposal your one concern now will be to get it accepted and implemented. If you are confident that you have a good idea and have written it up persuasively and positively then you are well on the way to success. However, to give yourself the final edge you will need to concentrate a little on the presentation of your document. A well presented proposal will not make up for poor content but a poorly presented one will be a black mark against the content before it has even been read. To give your

proposal the best chance of acceptance you should pay equal attention to style and substance.

Looking at layout and format

The layout and format of your proposal will be responsible for creating first impressions, so it is important to get it right. The first thing to consider is the **typeface** that you are going to use. This will involve similar considerations as for report writing (see Chapter 2) but with one difference. Since a proposal is, in some ways, a more informal and innovative type of document you do not have to stick to a conservative typeface. Try experimenting with the selection on your word processor or desk top publishing package until you think you have found one with the right image. Do not go over the top, though – you should allow yourself a degree of artistic licence, but not too much. Figure 6 shows a small selection of typefaces.

The next item to consider is the **format** of your proposal. It should start with a clear contents page, listing all the items in the document. These should have numbers that correspond to the sections of the proposal. Each section of the proposal should be numbered and have a title. The title should be left aligned, in bold and at least four point sizes bigger than the body text. Sub-sections should be numbered

---

Proposals — This typeface is Amerigo

Proposals — This typeface is AvantGarde

Proposals — This typeface is FritzQuadrata

Proposals — This typeface is Georgia

Proposals — This typeface is Swiss721

Proposals — This typeface is Tahoma

Proposals — This typeface is VAGRounded

Fig. 6. A selection of typefaces

sequentially and the heading should be smaller than the main section heading. This is essentially the same format as for a report (see Figure 3 in Chapter 2) and makes it easy for readers when they are referring to a certain part of the proposal.

It is usually best to print your text on one side of the paper as this makes it easier for the reader. However, if you are concerned about saving paper then it can be printed on both sides (backed-up).

Cover and binding
The cover is the first part of the proposal that the reader will see so it should be clear, informative and professional looking. It should not be crowded with information, but the following items should be included:

- the title of the proposal
- a sub-title giving a bit more information about the project
- the names of the people/section who have written the proposal
- the date of publication.

The design will depend on the budget and whether the proposal is being printed in black and white or in colour. Although colour can provide a stronger visual impact, black and white can also be used to good effect. The golden rule is 'keep it simple'. Figure 1 in Chapter 2 shows cover styles for a report that would also be suitable for a proposal.

The final consideration is how to collate and bind the finished product. The options here include:

- stapling
- comb-binding
- saddle stitching
- glued edge
- folding (A3 folded to A4 size) or
- holes punched for a ring binder.

Try to find examples of all of these options to see which you think is most appropriate for your publication. Whatever you choose, make sure that there is still a wide left-hand margin in the final document.

SUMMARY

1. Brainstorming can be a good way to generate ideas for a proposal, but it depends largely on the individual. Some people thrive on this type of multi-directional, inclusive method of working while

others find it a bit intimidating. Choose a method to suit you and do not be influenced by others.

2. Be enthusiastic about promoting what is in your proposal – if you are not enthusiastic about it then you cannot expect anyone else to be either. But do not become pushy. There is a fine line between enthusiastic and arrogant.

3. Make an effort to include examples and quotes. The people reading the proposal will want to see hard evidence to back up what you say. If you can show them an example of where your idea has already worked effectively then this will be a big bonus.

ACTION POINTS

1. Take part in some practice brainstorming sessions to see if it suits your style.

2. Write down all of the main points and arguments of your proposal. Then go through them and discard any that you feel are not as strong as they could be.

3. Create a list of words and phrases that you think convey a positive and upbeat image. Then try and incorporate as many of them as possible into your proposal.

4. Make a list of any relevant experts that you know of. If necessary, contact them for information or a quote.

5. Work on a variety of designs for the cover of your proposal after all, this will be the first thing that the reader sees.

4

Standardising Business Letters

Business letters are usually the external version of memos – they are sent to a wide variety of customers and clients and without them the business world would certainly revolve a lot more slowly. They also cover an extensive range of topics, from simple requests for information to complicated explanations, so the business letter writer has to be able to amend and adapt his/her style accordingly.

FORMATTING LETTERHEADS

The first task when producing a business letter is to decide on the style of letterhead that you are going to use. In many cases this will follow the style adopted by your company or organisation. If you are creating a letterhead from scratch, a number of components need to be included:

- The company logo (Figure 7 shows a selection of styles for logos.)
- Your organisation's name.
- Your organisation's address.
- Your telephone, fax and email numbers.

All of these elements can be arranged in a variety of ways and Figure 8 illustrates some possible combinations for laying out a letterhead.

Using a logo

One of the most important elements of a letterhead is the **logo** and the way it is used. A logo is a symbol or icon that serves as a visual identifier for the organisation. A successful logo does not have to be complicated to be effective and some of the most memorable corporate logos have been simplicity itself: for example the McDonald's golden arches, the Shell logo and the Nike 'swoosh', which all benefit from being simple and instantly recognisable.

Logos can either be a symbol or a combination of the letters or initials from the organisation's name. If the latter is used then try not to be too clever with it – if it is too complicated then people may not

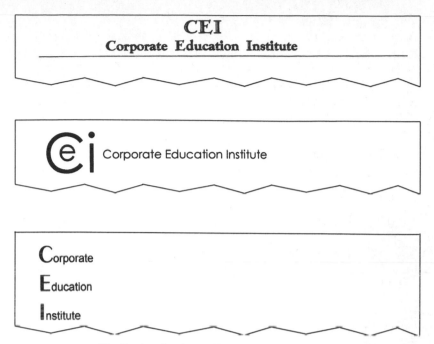

Fig. 7. A selection of logos for a letterhead.

understand what you are trying to do. Using colour is a good idea
with a logo (and some logos are recognisable by their colours alone)
but it is best to limit the number of colours used to two or three at
the most.

Incorporating a logo into your letterhead
There are a number of ways in which a logo can be positioned in a
letterhead and the most common are:

* left-aligned
* centred
* right-aligned.

Whatever alignment you choose for your letterhead you should
stick to it and use it in this way consistently. You should also use it
in close proximity to your organisation's name and the two should
ultimately be viewed as one unit. When designing the relationship
between the logo and the company name there should be a good bal-
ance between these two elements and they should complement one
another so that recipients will know at once where the letter comes
from.

Making your letterhead effective

Apart from the logo and the company name the rest of the information on the letterhead has to be clear and easily accessible. Clients or customers should not have to search around the page to find a return address or phone number. If they do, then the most likely result is that they will give up and turn to another company which takes the trouble to present such information in a more professional manner.

Traditionally, information such as a return address, telephone number, fax number, date, and reference numbers are placed in the top right corner of the page on a business letter. The reason for this is that it is well separated from any other part of the letter and therefore easy to spot. It also leaves the area opposite free for the name and address of the recipient (it is particularly useful to have the recipient's information here so that it can be seen when folded and placed in a window envelope). However, for design purposes it is permitted to move these elements around on the page – see Figure 8.

PRODUCING AN EFFECTIVE INTRODUCTION

The introduction to a business letter can serve several functions:

- It can acknowledge previous correspondence.
- It can detail the contents of the letter.
- It can make a request for further information.

Just as with the introduction to any other type of writing, the first paragraph of a business letter has to make the reader want to keep reading. If the introduction is vague, long-winded or confusing then the rest of the letter may be ignored, no matter how riveting it is.

Acknowledging previous contact

The first thing to do in an introduction is to acknowledge any previous contact or correspondence that you have had with the person you are writing to. This could be in the form of, 'Thank you for your letter of 1 August regarding our forthcoming marketing campaign' or slightly more detailed such as, 'I am writing as a result of our telephone conversation on 1 August during which you expressed various concerns about the targeting of our "Whiter than White" marketing campaign'. It is important to be brief and precise with these details: the recipient should know what you are talking about so you do not need to bore them by going over old ground.

When you are referring to a previous letter, telephone call or meet-

Cei Corporate Education Institute

Ian Wilson
Managing Director
Education House
14-18 High Street
Learning Town
LT23 4LL

Telephone: 01224 79882
Fax: 01224 79888
Email: cei@education.co.uk

(1)

Cei Corporate Education Institute

Ian Wilson, Managing Director, Education House, 14-18 High Street, Learning Town, LT23 4LL

Telephone: 01224 79882; Fax: 01224 79888; Email: cei@education.co.uk

(2)

CORPORATE EDUCATION INSTITUTE

Education House, 14-18 High Street, Learning Town, LT23 4LL

Telephone: 01224 79882, Fax: 01224 79888

Email: cei@education.co.uk

Web Site: www.ceieducation.htm

Managing Director: Ian Wilson. Directors: Brian Wilson, Sandra Wilson, Paul Wilson

(3)

Fig. 8. Three ways of laying out a letterhead.

ing always include the day and, if applicable, the other people who were involved. This way a busy customer or client will be able to place you and your company more quickly rather than becoming frustrated by having to look back through his or her records.

Summarising the contents

One of the main tasks of an introduction is to summarise what is in the body of the letter. Just as a screenwriter creates a summary of his film to 'pitch' to producers, so a letter introduction acts as a mini advertisement for what is to come. In this respect your opening should be:

- punchy
- persuasive
- concise
- informative.

If the introduction is well written then the recipient should not be taken by surprise by anything that appears later in the letter. In some cases it may be advisable to write the body of the letter first and then use this to form the introduction. This way you do not have to worry about straying from the arguments that are set out initially. Since clarity and brevity are two of the secrets to effective business writing, introductions do not have to be long-winded to be effective. The following example shows an introduction that covers all of the main points and then prepares the reader for the body of the letter.

'Thank you for your letter of 1 August and the points you made about our forthcoming marketing campaign, which begins on 1 October. I take on board what you say about the campaign being targeted at some of the wrong groupings. I have spoken to my manager about this and we feel that, with your help, there are a number of things we can do to improve the campaign's effectiveness.'

This shows the recipient that their letter has been read and acted upon constructively. It prepares them for the forthcoming points in the body of the document. Contrast this with the following introduction:

'I have just looked at your recent letter and it seems that you have some problems with our marketing campaign that will be beginning soon. Personally, I think that the campaign, which we have been working on for several months in various forms, is excellent and I fail to see how what you suggest will improve matters. I have seen the campaign develop from its early stages and, if I may, I would like to give you a detailed history of it so you may be able to understand our position better.'

This example not only displays an intransigent and arrogant position by the writer but it is also vague and is unlikely to inspire the recipient to read on, unless it is out of some kind of masochistic delight.

When you are writing an introduction you should always try and maintain a professional and friendly tone, even if the letter is going to contain bad or unwanted news. Use the introduction to get the recipient on your side rather than to set out the parameters for a forthcoming battle. If you start out badly then things will only get worse.

GETTING THE TONE RIGHT

Making it concise and professional

Professional people involved in business are generally very busy and they have a great number of demands on their time. Therefore it is important that when they see your letter they make time in their busy schedule to read it. This means that it not only has to *look* effective but it has to *be* effective too. Even if you are writing to someone you know well it is best not to waste time with a lot of small talk and generalities. The most important functions of business letters are:

- To convey the information as quickly and as clearly as possible.
- To let the reader know what to do if they need more information.
- To inform the reader of any benefits that may accrue to them.
- To develop a trusted business relationship

Drawing up a structure

The best way to achieve a productive business letter is to plan it carefully. The first step in doing this is to jot down what you want from the letter – are you explaining, persuading or selling? Then write out the number of paragraphs that you are going to use and what the purpose of each one is. (Remember to make sure that all of the paragraphs are linked together and that they follow a logical order.)

Good writing of any kind is rarely achieved at the first time of asking and this is particularly true when writing a business letter. Indeed, it would be a mistake to agonise over a single draft, in the hope that you will be able to get every word right first time. Try writing at least two drafts before you attempt the final version. In the first draft you should follow your structure, but the main aim is to get the words onto the paper. Then, with the second draft you can edit, re-write and amend your text. Keep doing this until you are completely satisfied with the result. The more experienced you become at writing then the better you will get at 'feeling' when something is right or not. If you have any nagging doubts, then keep re-writing the relevant parts.

Writing for your audience

Although business letters are frequently thought of as a single generic style of writing they can appear in a wide range of styles. This is because the audience for business letters is wide and varied. For instance, a bank or building society could write business letters to all of the following groups of people:

- children
- single people
- young married couples
- self-employed business people
- pensioners.

All of these groups would require a very different approach and this illustrates the importance of knowing your audience when you are writing a business letter. You should always be flexible and be ready to adapt your style accordingly.

Points to bear in mind

- Use of **language**. If you are writing for a young or youthful audience then you could probably get away with a more informal style. However, this will depend largely on the topic about which you are writing.

- The **size of type**. It is a fact of life that as we get older, our eyesight deteriorates. So if you are writing to a group of people in the over 60s age bracket then you should adjust your type size accordingly. Use at least 11 point and preferably 12 point if you want to get your message across and not cause irritation and annoyance.

- The style of **typeface**. This can have a considerable effect on the reader of a business letter. Some typefaces, such as Century Gothic, convey a modern, energetic image, while others, like Times Roman, give a more traditional look. Some typefaces can also be used for specific reasons. For instance, Courier is often used by charities when they send out pro forma letters because it gives the appearance of being typewritten and is therefore not as hi-tech and flashy.

IDENTIFYING A COMFORTABLE STYLE

On the surface it would seem that having your own style is one of the easiest things to achieve in writing. We are all different, we all write differently, so therefore we all have own styles. Right? Well, not exactly. Sometimes people feel that they have to write in a certain way to conform to the genre in which they are communicating. This is particularly true of business writing when people often feel that they have to be serious, convoluted and dull, just because they are writing on a business topic. The truth is that a natural, individual style can be a lot more effective than a stilted, derivative one.

Confidence is the key

The best way to find a comfortable writing style is to feel confident about your own abilities. This does not mean thinking you can do everything well first time, but rather confidence that comes through practice and hard work. The more that you write then the better you will become, providing that you plan your work carefully, know what you are writing about and take care to analyse your work once you have finished. As you become more confident you will then feel more secure in expressing yourself in your own style and this will add your own mark to your business writing. Do not be afraid to add a personal touch because this can make all the difference in the sometimes staid world of business communication – even businessmen have a sense of humour.

Exercising your writing muscles
Except for the gifted few, good writing is achieved through practice rather than just sheer inspiration and talent. Try some of the following exercises to expand your business writing repertoire and to see if you can identify a personal style with which you feel comfortable.

- Pick a topic and then draft a letter on it from three different viewpoints: yourself, the customer and the managing director. Imagine how people in different positions approach the same issue.

- Draft three business letters in different styles: convoluted, lighthearted and aggressive. Pick out the good points from each style (if any) and analyse what makes them effective.

- Collect a selection of business letters and try and copy the styles, to see which ones you like or dislike.

- Try and write the sort of letter you would like to receive yourself.

Analysing the results
One of the best ways to gain confidence from your writing is to get a positive reaction from the recipient. Always try and follow up your business letters by seeing if they achieved the desired result. For instance, if you have asked the recipient to respond in some way, and they do, then it can be assumed that the letter was effective and achieved its aim. Although this may not seem like a major triumph it should be remembered that in the business world people have a lot of pressures on their time and so getting a reply to a letter should not be underestimated.

If you do get a positive response to a piece of correspondence then let people know about it. They will then have more confidence in your abilities, which in turn should give you a boost.

FOLLOWING CONVENTIONS

Standards for business letter have evolved over the years. So what may have been acceptable 30 or 40 years ago is now seen as archaic and out of date. There are a number of areas that are subject to changes in fashion and style:

- the greeting
- the topic identifier
- indents
- spacings
- the ending.

Choosing the right greeting
The greeting on a business letter is one of the most contentious parts of the whole document. Do you use Dear Sir/Dear Sirs/Dear Sir or Madam? The answer is, ideally, none of them. These are traditionally used if you do not know the name of the recipient but in the modern business world they now seem old-fashioned and can cause offence or irritation – after all, who wants to be addressed as 'Dear Sir or Madam'?

To overcome the need to use Dear Sir, or any of its variants, the simplest answer is to find out the name of the person you are writing to. You may be able to do this by looking at some previous correspondence and getting their name from this or you could telephone the company's switchboard and ask the name of their marketing director/travel editor/or chief executive. For the price of a phone call you will then be able to open your letter on a personal note rather than revealing that you cannot take the time and effort to find out the name of the person with whom you want to communicate.

Using Mr, Mrs, Miss or Ms

Another bone of contention is the use of a title, particularly with women, where they can be addressed in a variety of different ways. Again, a simple telephone call can establish what the person's preferred method of address is. Alternatively, you can leave out the title altogether. This is becoming increasingly common in business correspondence: instead of Dear John or Dear Mr Smith you could address them as Dear John Smith, and Dear Mrs Brown would become Dear Margaret Brown. Although this is considered to be a little awkward in some quarters it is a good way to ensure that people are not addressed by the wrong title.

Never assume that you know the sex of a recipient and therefore choose a title accordingly – Chris Jones could be either male or female.

Identifying your topic

The topic identifier is a relatively recent addition to business correspondence and it acts as a heading to let the reader know what the letter is about. It comes between the greeting and the first line of the introduction and is usually in bold and/or uppercase type. An example of a topic identifier would be:

Improvements to marketing campaign or **WHITER THAN WHITE PROPOSALS**

The topic identity should be able to stand on its own and effectively explain the subject of the letter. If the identifier needs to be clarified or expanded upon then it is not doing its job properly and should be rewritten.

Dealing with indents

The days of indenting paragraphs in business letters are now long gone. Each paragraph should be flush with the left-hand margin and either aligned on the right or left 'ragged' (*ie* justified or unjustified). A justified paragraph looks more formal, while an unjustified one gives a more relaxed and informal appearance. Choose the one more suitable to the subject of your letter and the recipient.

The only time to use indents is when you are including an example or a long quote in your letter. In this instance the indented text should be at least a centimetre in from both sides of the text. In general it is desirable to have generous margins on all sides of the letter: it is no use cramming everything onto one page if no one is going to read it. If you have to, then use a second sheet of paper – it will be more productive in the long run.

Using spacings

Text in a business letter should be single-spaced, with one line space between each paragraph. Also, it is widely accepted that there is only one space after a full stop and the beginning of the next sentence. In the past, typists had been taught to insert two or three spaces before a new sentence but this is now considered unnecessary and one usually suffices. Similarly, after a comma there should only be one space before the start of the next word.

Finishing professionally

It is always good to end on a professional note and this can be done through the correct use of the ending. If you used the recipient's name at the beginning of the letter, eg Dear John Smith, then the ending should be 'Yours sincerely'. If the letter began 'Dear Sir or Madam' then the accepted ending is 'Yours faithfully'. Increasingly in modern business letter writing the sender adds a line before the ending such as 'Best wishes' or 'Please give me a call if I can provide you with any more information'. Although this does not add much to the content of the letter it is a way of generating a feel-good element.

PSs can be used in business letters, but it is rare – it can be unprofessional to show that you have forgotten something or not planned your text properly. Figure 9 shows a professional and well laid-out letter.

SUMMARY

1. Business letters still have an important part to play in the face of greater competition from new technology. They are still the most commonly accepted form of business communication and are likely to remain so for many years to come.

Cei Corporate Education Institute

Ian Wilson
Managing Director
Education House
14-18 High Street
Learning Town
LT23 4LL

Telephone: 01224 79882
Fax: 01224 79888
Email: cei@education.co.uk

24 May 1999

Elizabeth Simmons
Head Teacher
Southside High School
London EH14 9TT

Dear Elizabeth Simmons

Computer Learning Solutions

Thank you very much for your letter of 20 May regarding my earlier enquiry about the possibility of our company providing your school with some computer-generated learning aids.

I am glad that you think the proposal is one worth considering and so I would be happy to come to your school and give you, and any of your colleagues who may be interested, a demonstration of our products. This should take approximately one hour and then I will answer any questions that may arise.

You may also be interested to know that in addition to our standard packages we can also produce learning software that is tailored specifically for one school or one range of pupils.

I hope this is of use to you and if you would like to give me a call on the above number then I will be delighted to arrange a time for a visit.

I look forward to hearing from you again soon.

Yours sincerely

Ian Wilson

Fig. 9. An example of a well laid-out letter.

2. All your business letters should follow a similar style of presentation – this conveys an image of professionalism and continuity.

3. You do not have to stick to a dry business style of writing: incorporate some of your own style, but do not get too carried away and remember that it is a professional piece of communication.

ACTION POINTS

1. Design a number of different letterheads to see which one looks the best for your purpose.

2. Find out if your organisation has a house style for the presentation of letters. If so, then make sure you stick to it.

3. Write down all of the different groups of people with whom you deal. Be aware of the need for a different style of writing for each group.

4. Always try and find out the full name of anyone you are writing to.

5. Make sure your letters look professional as well as sound professional.

5

Mastering Memos

If there is one item of business writing that best sums up office life then it is the memo. Memos (short for memorandum) are formal business communications that are traditionally used for everything from arranging meetings to proposing new business procedures. They can be long or short, simple or detailed, but they are still the epitome of administrative life in the workplace. Or rather, they used to be.

ASSESSING THE ROLE OF THE MEMO

With the advent of personal computers and improvements in communications technology the position of the humble memo in the office hierarchy is being seriously threatened. Answering machines, voice mail and email have all contributed to the decline in use of internal memos. In many ways this is a good thing because memos are often used unnecessarily – somehow people think their message will be more important if it is produced in a memo.

When not to use them

When you are thinking about sending a memo ask yourself if this really is the best way to get your message across. It may be worth considering these three alternatives:

- **Email**. In some people's eyes the equivalent of the modern memo. Email can convey exactly the same message, to the same group of people, as a memo, only it does it instantly. You do not have to wait to have the message printed and distributed, as with a memo. (See Chapter 10 for a more detailed look at email.)

- **Telephone**. This is still one of the best ways to pass on information quickly, plus it has the added advantage of involving one-to-one human contact. The drawback is that there is usually no record of what was said. So if you arrange a meeting over the phone and the other parties do not turn up it can be difficult to determine who is at fault.

- **Face-to-face**. As with the telephone this involves human contact which can be a good way of avoiding any confusion that may arise from a written communication. But there is still the problem of having no written record of what was said and it is not always logistically possible for people in large organisations to meet face-to-face.

When to use them

Despite the competition that it faces from the new boys on the communications block, the memo still has an important role to play in the workplace. There will always be people who do not like or understand computers and they will continue to favour paper memos over the flasher email versions. As long as this works within the organisation then this is fine. People sending memos should be aware that their information will travel more slowly than the electronic variety but if this is not a problem then it is best to live and let live.

The one instance when it is preferable to send a memo is when you need to have documentary evidence of what was said. This is possible with email to a point but there is always the chance that the computer system will crash, deleting everything on it in the process. If you want to have proof of having arranged a meeting, or booking your annual leave, then the best way to do this is with a memo. You should file any memos you send or receive and keep them until the relevant event has passed (or beyond).

TAKING CARE WHEN COPYING

The most contentious aspect of memo writing is the question of whom, if anyone, should it be copied to. The dreaded 'cc' is the one part of a memo that can turn an apparently innocuous communication into a minefield. The rules for copying memos are far from set in concrete but in general a memo can be copied to any parties who may have an interest in the item that is being discussed. This could include:

- Your immediate superior, so they know what you are doing.

- The superior of the person to whom you are sending the memo.

- Any section that may be affected directly or indirectly by the memo. For instance, if you are sending a memo to a colleague urging them to get linked to the Internet then the memo should be copied to your IT division because this will have technical implications for them.

Copying with finesse

Human nature being what it is there are a number of ways people can take offence in relation to the copying of memos. The most obvious is when you copy a memo to the recipient's immediate superior. Although this is logical and courteous the recipient could view it as an attempt to undermine them and show them up in front of their boss. If you think this might be the case it is worth telling the recipient beforehand who it is being copied to. This means that they know what to expect and shows that you are being completely open with them.

Conflict could also arise if you are sending a number of copies to a group of related parties and inadvertently leave someone off the list. This is usually the result of a genuine mistake, but try explaining that to the person who was left off. If you want to leave someone out of the loop deliberately then you should think carefully about who will have access to the memo and if they are likely to show it to the third party. Openness is usually the best policy if you want to avoid upsetting your colleagues with your memos.

FORMATTING THE CONTENT

The format for a memo is usually clearly defined and is made up of certain fixed features. The content on the other hand is up to the writer. By definition, it is serious and business-like but there are always ways to add a little bit of individuality, which may be the difference between the memo being read or filed straight into the wastepaper basket.

Following a format

The format for a business memo has become formalised over the years and it consists of two main parts:

1. The header information.
2. The body of the memo.

Creating a header

The header information is the first thing that the reader sees and it should give them all the information they need about the origin of the memo. This includes:

- the date

- the recipient(s)
- the author of the memo
- the subject matter
- the people to whom the memo has been copied.

The header does not have to be flashy or complicated, just straightforward and informative. Most word-processing package have templates for creating memos or else there will be a house style that should be followed. Figure 10 shows various layouts for memos.

Writing the body
The body of the memo is where you get down to the business of getting your message across. Although a memo may be a relatively short item of communication it still needs to be well thought out and thoughtfully written. In the workplace most managers see dozens of pieces of paper every day and in order to get yours noticed you will have to give careful thought to the following areas:

- **Planning**. Even if you are only writing a short memo to arrange a meeting you will still need to plan what you want to say and how you want to say it. You will need to consider the position of the recipient of the memo, the reaction that you are aiming to get from them and the tone of language that will best serve your purposes.

- **Drafting**. There is nothing wrong with writing a few draft versions of your memo. This will enable you to get your thoughts into a logical order and clarify what you want to say. With the first draft you can put down all of the ideas and issues that you think may be relevant. Then, with subsequent drafts you can edit this down to the most polished version you can achieve. When you reach the final draft make sure that each paragraph follows on naturally from the previous one and that the overall memo actually makes sense.

- **Writing**. The writing style and tone of a memo is important because you want to convey the right image to the reader. This means that your style in a memo to the managing director will probably be different to one you send to your friend in another department. Whatever the tone of the memo the style will always be your own. After all, a memo is from an individual and so there is nothing wrong if it has a bit of that individual in the style of writing. This does not mean you can go wild and start littering your memos with informal statements and colloquialisms. As with other business

Memorandum

DATE: 1 November 1999
TO: Bill Cameron
FROM: Mary Martin
RE: Annual Staff Party
CC: Stuart Reed

Bill

I am delighted to let you know that the Chief Executive has once again agreed to sponsor a staff party this Christmas, in recognition of everyone's hard work during the year.

(1)

Memo

To: Bill Cameron
From: Mary Martin
CC: Stuart Reed
Date: 1 November 1999
Re: Annual Staff Party

Bill

I am delighted to let you know that the Chief Executive has once again agreed to sponsor a staff party this Christmas, in recognition of everyone's hard work during the year.

(2)

INTEROFFICE MEMORANDUM

TO: BILL CAMERON
FROM: MARY MARTIN
SUBJECT: ANNUAL STAFF PARTY
DATE: 1 NOVEMBER 1999
CC: STUART REED

Bill

I am delighted to let you know that the Chief Executive has once again agreed to sponsor a staff party this Christmas, in recognition of everyone's hard work during the year.

(3)

Fig. 10. Three ways of laying out a memo.

writing your style of memo should be economical and clear. Think carefully about what you want to say before you start writing and then say it in short, clear sentences and paragraphs. If you do this then you will have an effective memo that still retains some of your own character.

AVOIDING ANTAGONISTIC MEMOS

Coping with memo conflict

The main functions of memos are:

* to request something ('As a result I feel it would be useful if we could be allocated a fax machine')

* to highlight a certain issue ('So, as you can see, the unreliability of the heating system is causing genuine problems in our section')

* to make an arrangement ('I would therefore be grateful if you could all attend the training course on Monday').

However, because memos can be written relatively quickly a number of pitfalls can occur.

Writing in the heat of the moment

If all memos were written when the writer was feeling cool, calm and collected then there would be less antagonism in the workplace. Unfortunately, many memos are produced when the writer is feeling tired, distracted, frustrated, angry or harassed. This inevitably leads to memos that are written in the heat of the moment, leading to nasty cases of 'memo rage', where the prevailing mood of the writer is conveyed on paper and then sent without a second thought. The recipient therefore receives a communication that comes across as hostile, confusing or irritating.

In this situation it is vital for the writer either to wait an hour or two before they write the memo, or to write it, put it aside and then re-read it an hour or two later, before it is sent. It is amazing how our moods and feelings can change in this short period of time. What may have seemed like a succinct and powerful memo when it was written in a moment of anger may appear irrational and downright rude when read in the cold light of day. Always look at your memos with an objective eye and imagine the effect they are going to have on the recipient: one memo sent in anger could result in a deluge of irate correspondence.

Misinterpretation
If the recipient of a memo does not understand its meaning then this could have serious consequences for the organisation. If this happens then the blame lies firmly on the writer of the memo. If a memo is about a particularly complicated subject or is likely to be misinterpreted then the writer will need to be extra careful with its construction. In order to prevent any embarrassing cases of misinterpretation the following points could be considered:

• Use a separate paragraph for each point or idea.

• Always use a new paragraph for any new information.

• Read over the memo to make sure it makes sense to you.

• Give the memo to someone else and then ask him or her what it is about.

• Be ruthless in editing any parts of the memo that could cause confusion or doubt.

• Never underestimate people's capacity for taking things the wrong way.

• Ask the recipient to telephone you if there are any points that they would like to clarify.

Misplaced humour or flippancy
Humour in any type of business writing is always a contentious issue. What one person finds uproariously funny, another may find offensive and objectionable. Office humour does not usually translate very well onto paper, particularly as the mood of the recipient may be considerably different to that of the writer. If you include humour in a memo to a superior or someone you do not know very well then the potential for embarrassment is huge. Even if you include a humorous remark in a memo to a friend who you know will find it funny, this too could backfire: if someone else reads the memo they may not see it in the same light.

As a rule it is best to steer clear of humour and flippant remarks in memos altogether. The chances of it improving the memo are slim and it is much more likely to convey a negative image. However, if you do use humour in a memo, make absolutely certain that you avoid all of the following areas:

- sex
- gender
- race
- politics
- other members of the office.

Office harassment and bullying is an important issue in the modern workplace and if a supposedly humorous remark is taken the wrong way then it could result in very serious consequences for the individual and company involved.

DEALING WITH BAD NEWS

Leaving it out

Unfortunately, not all memos contain news of pay bonuses and extra days' holidays. There are times when there is bad news to communicate – sometimes a memo is the best way of doing this and sometimes it is not. As a general rule, the more serious the news, then the less suitable it is for a memo. For instance, if an employee receives a memo saying, 'You are going to be made redundant on Friday' they may despair and head for the nearest window ledge. In cases such as this it is better to pass on the information face-to-face so at least there is some human contact and an explanation can be given.

Memos can be a very impersonal method of communication and the means of conveying bad news should always be considered as well as the actual subject matter.

Softening the blow

Certain types of bad news are inevitable in business life, even if it is only to tell someone that they are not going to be moved into their own office. At times like this it is diplomatic to break the bad news in as understanding a way as possible. This usually means opening the memo with a piece of positive information and keeping the negative side of things until further into the document. So, using the example of the new office, an unsympathetic memo could read:

> Unfortunately there has been a reorganisation of the second floor and so it is no longer possible to provide you with your own office.

This is a bad memo because not only is it abrupt, but it also gives no reason for the change in the accommodation plans. In this example a much better way to approach the subject would be to give the individual some praise to begin with, then explain the situation and then finish on a positive note:

I have noticed in recent weeks that you have been working in rather cramped and overcrowded conditions. Despite this I am aware of the high level of productivity that you and your team have been maintaining. Unfortunately, due to an expansion in our marketing division you may have to persevere with these conditions for a few more weeks at least, until we can find you a new office. I appreciate the patience that you have shown and I am sure you will take this in your stride as you seem to do with most other inconveniences.

This shows the recipient that they are valued and that management understands the problems that exist.

Whenever you have to convey bad news in a memo always try to find something positive to say too. There is nothing more depressing than being handed a memo that is filled with bad news and negative comments.

SUMMARY

1. A memo is not always the best way to make arrangements or pass on items of information. Look at the information and the people to whom you want to communicate it and then assess the best way of doing it. A memo may be the answer but also look at alternatives such as the telephone and email.

2. Memos still have an important role to play in office life. They are an excellent way of maintaining written proof of ideas, suggestions and arrangements.

3. Memos *can* be used to announce bad or negative news, but only moderately bad news. If there is something really serious to announce then this should be done in person or in a personal letter. This is a matter of judging each case on its merits.

ACTION POINTS

1. Have a policy for when you do, and do not, copy memos to other people. Always be aware of the sensitivities that this involves.

2. Use a format that is simple and effective. Make sure that all of the relevant information is easily visible to the recipient.

3. Create a memo template so that you do not have to start from the beginning each time. Most word processing packages will be able to provide you with ready-made templates.

4. Never write, and send, a memo in the heat of the moment. Always give yourself a couple of hours for rational reflection.

5. Be careful with humour. Unless you know the recipient very well, it could backfire.

6

Writing and Designing Newsletters

It is a fact of business life that no one ever has the luxury of producing the office newsletter as his or her only task. Invariably the MD or Chief Executive decides that a publication for the organisation would be a good idea, and then promptly nominates someone to create it. Usually it is an employee who has shown a reasonable aptitude with the written word but other than that it could be someone from almost any part of the organisation. More importantly, it could be you.

Just as the editor, or editorial team, of an office newsletter will have several other aspects to their job, so too will producing the publication be a varied task. They will be expected to deal not only with the written aspect of the newsletter, but also with the following:

- layout and design
- commissioning articles
- finding news items
- producing the finished version.

All in all it is a challenging task, but, done well, it can do wonders for your organisation – and also your own standing.

TACKLING LAYOUT AND DESIGN

Getting to grip with the basics

If you have never dealt with any layout or design then the whole concept may fill you with dread. But fear not! The basics are easy to grasp and once you have these you will be able to produce a professional-looking newsletter. Once you feel confident with this you will be amazed at how your hitherto undiscovered design talent will blossom.

If you are asked to design a newsletter or magazine as well as writing it, make sure you are provided with a suitable desk top publishing (DTP) package. The standards in the industry are *QuarkXpress* or *Adobe PageMaker* but these are both expensive. However, there are cheaper alternatives on the market such a *Microsoft Publisher*.

At a push, good quality word processing packages could be used but they do not offer the flexibility of a dedicated DTP program.

Deciding on a format
The first thing to decide is the format of your newsletter. The choice is fairly straightforward:

- A4
- tabloid.

Of the two, the first is the most common and the easiest to use. It allows for a manageable publication that is easy to work with from a design point-of-view. The tabloid format allows for slightly more flexibility but this is offset by its size and the implications this can have for printing.

Choosing a grid
Before you put any words onto paper you have to decide on the number of columns each page of your publication is going to have. This is known as the **grid** and once you have decided on it then it should be adhered to strictly. The number of columns will depend on the image you want to convey and the amount of confidence you have in your own design abilities. The four main choices are:

- One column. This is a very basic grid that is best used if you want to convey a serious, strait-laced image, or if you are not very confident about layout and design (see Figure 11a).

- Two column. This allows for more flexibility but still creates a solid and dependable image (see Figure 11b).

- Three column. This is one of the most versatile and popular grid formats. It is easy to combine text and graphics and can be used to convey a variety of images (see Figure 11c).

- Scholar's margin. This is a grid where one column is significantly narrower than the other. This is ideal if you want to include notes or additional material at the side of the text – the column is also sometimes called a sidebar. This is a popular format, particularly for technical publications (see Figure 11d).

Once you have chosen the type of grid you want to use you should create a template to work from. You can experiment with your grid specifications but it is important to leave generous margins around

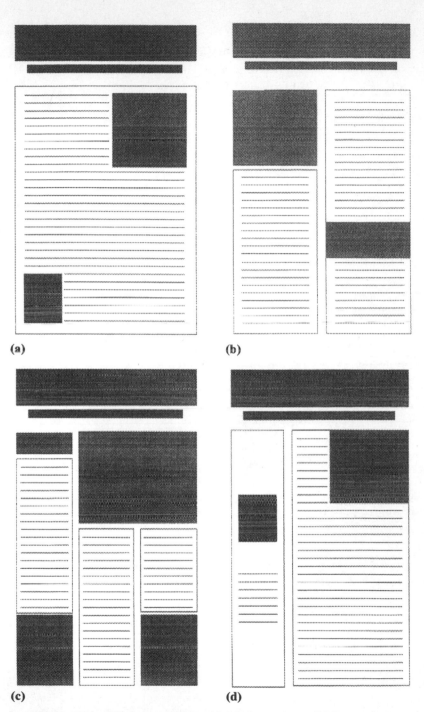

Fig. 11. Four different types of grid (a) One column (b) Two column
(c) Three column (d) Scholar's Margin.

the outside of the page and also between the columns. Once you have decided on your specifications, write them down on a style sheet so that other people could use it if necessary.

Nameplate
The nameplate is a fixed feature of any newsletter and consists of two important elements:

• The name of the publication

• A brief strap-line describing the newsletter, *eg* 'The newsletter of Worldwide Publishing. Issue 4, June 1999'.

These two elements should always be kept together and once you have chosen their style and position, stick to it. Examples of nameplates are shown in Figure 12.

Masthead
Like the nameplate, the masthead is a fixed element in the design of your newsletter. It is a box of information that expands on what has been said on the nameplate and can include some of the following:

• the address of the business
• the editor/editors of the newsletter
• the purpose of the publication
• deadline dates.

The masthead can be placed in a variety of positions within the publication but generally it appears on the front, inside front or back page. Experiment with the style of your masthead but, as with the nameplate, once you have a position for it treat this as a set element. Examples of mastheads are shown in Figure 13.

Note: The term masthead is often used instead of nameplate.

WORKING WITH TEXT AND GRAPHICS

Once the elements of your grid, nameplate and masthead are in place you can then start to think about the style of the words you are going to put in your publication.

Choosing body text
The body text for your publication will be made up of typefaces and fonts. A typeface is a family of type styles, *eg* Times New Roman, and a font is a particular member of that family, *eg* Times New Roman

in-house news

The newsletter of Worldwide Publishing. Issue 4, June 1999.

In-House News

The newsletter of Worldwide Publishing. Issue 4, June 1999.

In-house news

The newsletter of Worldwide
Publishing. Issue 4, June 1999.

in-house news

The newsletter of Worldwide Publishing. Issue 4, June 1999.

Fig. 12. Sample of nameplates.

In-House News is the staff newsletter for Worldwide Publishing, 87–95 High Street, Write Town. Telphone 456–8883. Fax. 456-8888

In-House News is produced and designed internally and printed by Graphics One Printers.

Articles and views for In-House News are always welcome and prospective contributors should contact the editor in Room 100, Ext. 1234.

In-House News is the staff newsletter for
Worldwide Publishing, 87–95 High Street, Write Town.
Telephone 456–8883. Fax. 456–888. In-House News is produced and
designed internally and printed by Graphics One Printers. Articles and
views for In-House News are always welcome and prospective contributors should contact the editor in Room 100, Ext. 1234.

In-House News is the staff newsletter for Worldwide Publishing, 87-95 High Street, Write Town. Telephone 456–8883. Fax. 456–8888

● ●

In-House News is produced and designed internally and printed by Graphics One Printers.

● ●

Articles and views for In-House News are always welcome and prospective contributors should contact the editor in Room 100, Ext. 1234.

Fig. 13. Sample mastheads.

Bold. Technically, you should use the separate fonts for styles such as bold and italics but in reality you can get away with using one type-face and then emboldening or italicising it.

The main choice when choosing body text is whether to have a serif or a sans serif typeface. The difference is that strokes of serif typefaces have slight loops at the end of them while sans serif ones are plain, *eg* S is a serif, and S is a sans serif. For body text of newsletters serif typefaces are more frequently used.

Whatever typeface you choose make sure you look at a whole page of it before you decide: some rounded typefaces may fill the page up too much while others could appear spindly. The size of your type-face should be no smaller than 9 point and no larger than 12 point.

Using headlines

Headlines should be set in a clear sans serif typeface that has an immediate visual impact. If you have more than one headline on a page, such as on a page of news items, you should make sure that the largest headline goes with the most important story and the other headlines are set in a smaller size. For instance, if you have three stories on a page then the main headline could be in 32 point, the next most important headline in 24 point and the final one in 18 point (Figure 14 illustrates a newsletter (reduced from A4) which shows the relative sizes of headlines.). There are a number of factors to consider if you want to produce effective-looking headlines:

1. Do not set headlines in all upper case type. Contrary to popular belief, this reduces readability rather than increasing it.

2. Never underline headlines. This is outdated, visually unattractive and unnecessary.

3. Make sure your headlines are big enough. They are the hook with which you are trying to catch the reader and you want to ensure that it is not missed.

4. Avoid setting headlines over dark colours, such as the background of a photograph, as this reduces readability considerably.

Setting alignment

An important factor in the final look of your publication will be the alignment of your text. It can either be left aligned or justified. If it is left aligned then the right-hand margin will look 'ragged', in the

in-house news

The newsletter of Worldwide Publishing. Issue 4, June 1999.

This headline is 32 point bold

Sub headings can also be included

This headline is 24 point

This headline is 18 point

Fig. 14. An example of relative headline sizes.

same way as a typewritten letter would. With a justified alignment both the right and the left-hand margins are straight. Your choice of alignment will depend on the tone you want to give your newsletter. Justified text, which has grown in popularity with the widespread use of PCs, gives a more ordered and sober look to blocks of text. Alternatively, if you want to create a more informal, relaxed image then left aligned is the best choice.

Including illustrations

A newsletter without illustrations is like a party political broadcast: informative but dull. There are several ways to illustrate your publication and all of them are worth consideration.

Photographs

Unless there is a reasonable budget with which to employ a freelance photographer, or buy picture from an agency, you may well be left to take photographs yourself. However, do not be put off because even with a standard 'point and press' camera good quality pictures can be produced if you follow a few simple steps:

- Make sure your subject fills the frame – you do not want readers squinting to see what is in the picture.

- Try and avoid static group shots where everyone stares rigidly at the camera. Ask your subjects to arrange themselves in informal positions or get them to do something active, even if it is just holding their arms in the air.

- People like to see pictures of other people, so restrain yourself from using too many scenic shots.

- When you are placing your photographs on the page try and make sure that people are 'looking in' towards the text rather than 'away' off the edge of the page.

- A bad photograph is worse than none at all – if this happens then look for an alternative.

Clip Art

Clip Art can add a strong visual element to your publication. But be warned, people are becoming very familiar with these images so they are best used sparingly. Try editing existing Clip Art images or you could buy discs of different images – there are numerous ones on the market, priced around £50.

Graphs and charts
These are particularly useful for financial and scientific information but if you are using graphs and charts then include as much colour as possible to attract the reader's attention.

Drawings
The availability of these may depend on your own abilities or else finding someone in your organisation who is a budding artist. Even if this is not immediately apparent at least you have the perfect platform to advertise for any willing candidates. It is well worth it too, because original artwork can have a great impact on a publication.

Getting the reader hooked
Once you feel confident about the textual and graphical aspects of your publication it is time to think about getting your audience to read what you put in it. A number of graphical devices can be used to increase readership but first it is important to understand how we look at page of a newsletter. Initially we view a page at the **optical centre**, which is above and to the left of the actual centre. We then scan down the page in a lazy Z pattern, which is known as eyeflow (see Figure 15). It is the job of the designer to catch the reader's eye as it scans down the page and this can be done in a number of ways.

- **Drop caps**. This is a device where the first letter of an article is considerably larger than the size of the body text so it draws the reader to the beginning of the article. DTP and word processing packages can insert drop caps automatically and they can increase readership by up to 20%. No more than three drop caps per page should be used, as this will give a cluttered appearance.

- **Pull quotes**. These are lines or sentences of text enlarged in the body text. This not only has the effect of highlighting an important issue in the article, it also breaks up the body text. Wherever possible, you should try and avoid large swathes of unbroken text.

- **Sidebars**. These are pieces of additional information that appear outwith the main article. They can be straight text or bulleted or numbered lists.

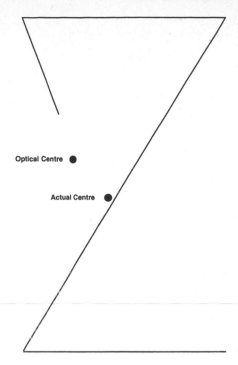

Fig. 15. An example of the optical centre and eyeflow.

- **Reverses**. This is when a word or short headline is highlighted by printing it in white on a dark background. These should be used sparingly or else they lose their effect and become intrusive.

- **Lines or rules**. These are a great way of breaking up articles and columns and can be used in a variety of styles.

Examples of these graphical devices are shown in Figure 16.

WRITING FEATURES AND COMMISSIONING ARTICLES

Feature writing is the central part of any newsletter. Features are articles that are usually one page or more (500 words+) and they can determine the success or otherwise of your publication. It is your job to get features into your publication and this can be done in two ways:

- commissioning them from other members of staff
- writing them yourself.

Drop caps can be used at the start of an article, to capture the reader's attention. No more than 3 drop caps should be used on one page. Some DTP programmes provide more artistic and ornate drop caps.

Pull quotes should be considerably larger than the body text and separated by lines or boxes.

Pull quotes should be considerably larger than the body text and separated by lines or boxes.

Sidebar information should be included in a plain or coloured box at the side of the main article. The format can be in plain text, bulleted lists or numbered lists. Two or three sidebars can be used per article.

Sidebar information should be included in a plain or coloured box at the side of the main article. The format can be in:
- plain text,
- bulleted lists or
- numbered lists.
Two or three sidebars can be used per article.

Sidebar information should be included in a plain or coloured box at the side of the main article. The format can be in:
1   plain text,
2   bulleted lists or
3   numbered lists.
Two or three sidebars can be used per article.

Reverses can be used for small amounts of text.

Or small headlines

Lines can be used in a variety of styles and weights

Fig. 16.   Examples of drop caps, pull quotes, sidebars, reverses and lines.

Identifying subject matter

If you want to encourage people to write features for your newsletter you will have to produce some editorial guidelines on subject matter – there is nothing worse than receiving an unsolicited feature and then having to tell the writer that it is unsuitable. Initially, you will have to decide whether you want articles exclusively about your organisation and the work it does or if you are also going to include general interest features. (This may depend on the powers that be, but whatever you decide you should fight your corner by putting together a proposal for editorial content. For more information about preparing proposals, see Chapter 3.)

Concentrating internally

If you want features that deal with issues within your organisation then you will have to think of topics that will interest your readers – and not just the same information that they see on a daily basis via notices, letters, memos and emails. Consider some of the following areas for possible features:

* **Stress** at work – how it relates to your organisation. Is it a stressful industry? Why do people suffer from stress? What is being done to improve the situation?

* The use of **new technology**. Does your company embrace new technology? What are the difficulties? Does the Internet have an impact on your industry? What future developments are likely?

* **Health and safety** issues. Do you suffer from Sick Building Syndrome? Do employees have RSI? Are there safety issues that need to be investigated?

* **Industrial espionage**. Is it applicable in your industry? Could it affect your business?

* **Training**. Does your company have any innovative training techniques? Are there are new options that could be considered? Find out and write about them.

* **Catering** facilities. Do you have them? Are they up to scratch? What do people think about them? Could they be improved?

With all of these topics it is the 'angle' you approach it from that will make it interesting rather than just the subject itself.

Broadening your outlook
If you want to include wide-ranging subject matter then you have greater scope for innovation but remember, each feature should serve a purpose in your publication – do not include something just because your best friend in another section has written it.

General features can include just about anything but try to keep them within the limits of current general interest issues:

- public transport issues
- the environment
- sport
- the media
- trends in television
- trends in fashion
- food and drink.

Other types of features
Features do not have to be straightforward articles about issues of the day. In order to vary the style of your publications it is worth-while to include some of the following styles of features:

- Interviews: the question and answer format works well in newsletters.

- Spotlight features: likes, dislikes *etc* of someone in the organisation.

- Guest column: people are usually delighted to write for office publications.

- '101 things you didn't know about . . .': a very popular format with tabloid newspapers and also a very effective one.

Understanding the anatomy of an article
No matter how industrious your readership is there will come a time when you will have to write features yourself. This need not be seen as a chore, especially once you have chosen your subject matter and know how a good feature is created. A feature is not an abstract, whimsical piece of prose that meanders along to its conclusions: it is a structured creature that is made up of carefully defined elements.

The introduction

This is the opening one or two paragraphs that draws the reader into the article, gets them hooked and encourages them to read on. It can be an historical reference ('Stress at work was evident even when the Egyptians were beginning the first pyramid'), an interesting statistic ('In the United States two per cent of workers suffer from stress due to the quality of the coffee in their office'), or an unusual incident that seems to have no immediate relevance to the topic of the article ('A flat battery was only the beginning of Mike's problems'). Whatever you do, do not start with a bland, boring statement such as, 'The Managing Director said that stress at work is becoming an increasing problem'. This is the kiss of death for any article. Instead, try to paint a picture with your introduction.

Key paragraph

This is a device that tells your reader what the article is about and the direction the rest of the feature is going to take, *eg* 'So even though stress is costing the economy millions of pounds a year there are ways to reduce this and create a more relaxed workforce. The latest stress-busting techniques from Japan bear more than a little investigation.'

Signposts

These are sentences or short paragraphs that alert the reader to the fact that you have finished one topic and are now taking a subtle change in direction, *eg* 'However, not everyone is convinced that the Huik-yen technique is all it is cracked up to be'. Each new issue or counter argument should be identified by a signpost.

Quotes

These are frequently used in features but often their full effect is lost. Quotes should convey emotions and feeling, not just bald facts that could be incorporated into another part of the feature. 'I concluded that stress could be reduced by lying down for ten minutes every day' could be improved by a quote such as, 'After my ten minute break I felt alive again! The blood was pumping, my mind was sharp and I was ready for action!' If you do want to change the wording of a quote, make sure you check first with the person you are quoting.

Linkback

In order to give your feature an effective ending, a linkback can be used. This is a sentence that takes the reader back to your introduction, thus giving a completed feel to the feature. Linkbacks for the above introductions could be, 'Impressive though the pyramids are, who knows what engineering marvels the Egyptians might have produced if they had had these modern relaxation techniques'. 'So the next time it is all getting too much at work you should perhaps gaze into the bottom of your coffee cup for a few moments.' 'As a result, Mike vowed to fix his battery first thing in the morning.'

Only use a linkback if it is appropriate. Do not put one in just because you like the device.

GATHERING NEWS ITEMS

Making it relevant

A vital element of any news story is that it is of interest to your readers. When you are looking for news items you should keep this at the front of your mind. You will probably need to consider two types of news stories:

1. **Internal stories** that deal with new initiatives within your organisation, notable achievements by members of staff and human interest stories – births, marriages, social events *etc*.

2. **External news events** that might affect your organisation. For instance, if you work for an oil company and war breaks out in an oil producing state then this will probably have an impact on your business.

   As well as reporting on past events, your news pages should also deal with up and coming events. The best type of news is an exclusive that has not appeared anywhere else in the organisation.

Finding news stories

Some news stories will be obvious ('MD gets a knighthood') but it will often be up to you to go out and find the news. Look for relevant stories in the local and national press and then follow them up. If you discover that a new shopping centre is being planned near your office then check it out. Contact your local council, any contractors involved, your local MP or anyone who might be able to throw some light on the subject. Most people are more than willing to talk to internal publications and it gives you important quotes. If you are interviewing people, try and make sure that you use a tape recorder. This ensures that there is never any doubt about who said what. Never make up quotes to suit your story.

All good reporters rely on sources to keep them supplied with information and stories, so ask your readers to keep an eye out for anything that might be suitable for your news pages. Even the most mundane fact can be made newsworthy if you have the right 'angle'.

Checking your sources

Inevitably when you are writing news stories you will be relying on a lot of different sources for information: newspapers, magazines, internal and external sources. Whatever facts and figures you are given, always check them with at least two other sources. This may mean a visit to the library or a few minutes on the telephone but it is well worth it to ensure that you do not print incorrect information. Errors are *always* spotted.

Writing news

When it comes to writing up your news stories you should follow the golden rule of the 5 Ws:

* who
* what
* where
* when
* why.

These should be included in the opening paragraph if possible, so the reader knows exactly what the news story is about, *eg*:

Alan Brown, the Managing Director of Independent Oil (**who**) received a knighthood (**what**) from the Queen at Buckingham Palace (**where**) on 1 March 1999 (**when**). The award was in recognition of his service to industry (**why**).

The second paragraph should then expand on these basic facts and then the story can branch out into more general information and background facts. Most stories should answer the question 'how?' as well.

News items should be concise and to the point. Keep to simple words and short sentences and paragraphs. If you think a news item is particularly interesting or noteworthy then expand it into a full-length feature rather than writing a long-winded news item.

PRODUCING THE FINISHED ARTICLE

After you have breathed a sign of relief at having found your news story, written and commissioned your features and put it all together with your DTP package, it is time to decide how you are going to print your masterpiece. There are two roads to go down, printing it internally or paying for an external printer to do the work. As with most things in life, the main consideration is cost. An external printer will offer the best service as far as quality is concerned but it will be more expensive. If you want to go down this route then you will probably need to persuade someone to part with the necessary sum. (See Chapter 3 Creating Proposals That Work to help you with this.)

Printing internally

If your organisation has a printing or a reprographics department then you can give serious consideration to producing your newsletter internally. If you have professional offset printing facilities at your disposal this would be perfect but it is more likely that it will be a question of photocopying. The options here are:

- black and white
- partial (or 'spot') colour
- full colour.

Unlike some of their predecessors, modern industrial photocopiers produce good quality in terms of finish and speed.

SUMMARY

1. Not every organisation needs a newsletter. If you feel that something is lacking in the communications within your company then a newsletter is a good idea. However, if there are already several avenues of communication then a newsletter might just lead to information overload. Having said that, employees usually complain of not enough information rather than too much.

2. It is better to produce a newsletter internally, in terms of cost. In terms of content and editorial control it is also a good idea to keep it in-house as you will know a lot more about the company than will an external organisation. However, if you want to avoid the workload of producing a newsletter it would be worthwhile considering an outside company, but you will pay for the privilege.

3. Involve as many people as possible in the newsletter to increase 'ownership' of your publication. Keep the editing and design to the editorial team but try and get as many contributed articles and news items as you can.

ACTION POINTS

1. Make sure you have a clear idea of the purpose of your news-letter. Is it to inform, or entertain, or both?

2. Have a specific hierarchy for who decides your editorial policy, who monitors what gets printed, who gets the credit for good work and who gets the blame for mistakes.

3. Conduct a staff survey to see if your publication is serving its purpose.

4. Create a list of areas for news stories, both internally and exter-nally.

5. Create some mock-up designs for your newsletter, to see which is the most appropriate for your organisation.

7

Using Forms, Surveys and Questionnaires

The production of office forms is one of the most notoriously difficult areas to control and monitor. In theory it is simple: one person, or department, is in charge or producing all the forms for the organisation and if anyone needs one they know where to go. In practice it is considerably harder: with the proliferation of word processors and desk top publishing packages it has become much easier for any employee to run off a form. This is particularly true for internal forms, when the author thinks it will be quicker and easier to produce their own form rather than go through the official channels.

PRODUCING AND CONTROLLING FORMS

The problem with forms

A form is a form is a form, isn't it? Well, no. Forms are a vital part of an organisation's workflow and it is important to have a clearly defined structure for the production of forms. If not, a variety of different styles of forms will appear from all parts of the office. This can cause a number of problems:

- **Poor corporate image**, particularly if people misuse the organisation's name or logo on a form.

- **Confusion and uncertainty**. Poorly designed forms can lead to problems for both the author and the recipient. This also applies if there are too many forms in existence. In China, a factory did an audit of all their forms and gave up after the total passed 1,600.

- **Waste of time**. Poorly designed forms invariably lead to mistakes being made when they are filled in. This in turn means that valuable time is wasted in trying to correct these mistakes. And since time is money in business, these can prove to be costly mistakes.

- **Frustration and stress**. Anyone who has ever grappled with a complicated or confusing form will know that it is not an enjoyable experience. Since there is enough stress in the modern workplace already this is one extra problem that is best avoided.

Creating a forms department

Centralising the production of forms
Rather than leaving forms to be created on an ad hoc basis it is worthwhile to consider creating a central forms department that is responsible for designing and producing all of your organisation's internal and external forms. While this is a noble ambition it is best to face the inevitable and accept the fact that some home-grown forms will always find their way into the system. The general remit for a forms department should include the following:

- Liaise with the generator of the form to find out what they want.

- Determine all of the people or areas that will be affected by the form.

- Design a draft version of the form.

- Show the draft to all interested parties for approval.

- Create the final version of the form and arrange for it to be printed and distributed.

- Collate a database of all new and existing forms.

Deciding on a house style
A house style is important for forms because it conveys a dependable, unified image. A customer filling in a series of forms will feel more comfortable if they all conform to the same style. A uniform style also portrays a strong corporate image and suggests that your organisation is well run and professional.

Before a house style is even considered the forms department should collect all of the forms (internal and external) that they can find throughout the organisation. This will probably reveal a startling array of the good, the bad and the ugly. This is a useful exercise because it will contribute to a forms database and also because it will give you a good idea of what looks good and what does not. Some points to bear in mind when producing a house style are:

- Use of the **company name** and logo. The style and colour of this should be consistent on all forms. In general it is a good idea to have it in the same style as appears elsewhere in the organisation such as on letterheads.

- **Typeface**. This should be clear and big enough to read. Although this may seem obvious, it is startling how many forms use a minute typeface in order to cram all of the information onto a page. This is unnecessary and counter-productive.

- Use of **reply boxes**. Should you use YES/NO boxes, blank boxes, shaded boxes, lined boxes or multiple-choice boxes? There is a place for all of them, if used correctly, and Figure 17 shows some examples.

- **Format**. A4 or A5, landscape or portrait?

Once a house style has been chosen it should be written up in a forms style guide. Ideally, then anyone could, if required, produce forms that are recognisable as coming from a particular organisation.

CONCENTRATING ON THE USER

Identifying your audience

As far as forms, surveys and questionnaires are concerned, the most important people in the equation are those who fill them in, the users. However, the people who design these documents often overlook this: all too frequently they produce something that they *think* the users will want, without actually having asked them. This results in the forms being filled in incorrectly, which is frustrating and time-consuming for both the user and the author of the form.

When someone asks you to produce a form or a questionnaire you should ask them two important questions:

1. Who is it for?
2. Have they been consulted about the document?

Once you have answers to these questions you can then begin to produce the form with some confidence. However, if there is any uncertainty about who the form is for, or what they want it for, then you should go back to square one. You should know the exact audience for the document because this could have a significant impact on the style and tone that you use. For instance the following groups

Do you use this service on a daily basis?   YES ☐ NO ☐

Please add any additional comments in this box:

```
┌─────────────────────────────────────┐
│                                     │
│                                     │
│                                     │
│                                     │
│                                     │
│                                     │
└─────────────────────────────────────┘
```

Please fill in this form using the reply boxes provided e.g.

Name | John Smith

Occupation | Surveyor

Please tick any of the following that apply:

Daily ☐   Weekly ☐   Monthly ☐   Rarely ☐   Never ☐

Fig. 17. Examples of reply boxes for forms.

would all have different needs for forms designed for them:

- **Members of the profession**. They will understand the jargon of their own profession. Therefore this can be used in the form or questionnaire, but other professional jargon may need to be explained more carefully.

- **Older people**. This will affect the layout of the document, because as we get older our eyesight deteriorates and so the form will have to be very clear, with as large a typeface as space will permit.

- **People with a low reading age**. A large proportion of the population has a below-average reading age and this should be taken into consideration. It is no use designing an impeccable looking document if the user cannot understand what it says.

- People filling in the form **by hand** or on a **typewriter or PC**. This can affect the layout because a form that can be filled in easily by hand may not accommodate the spacing for a typewriter or a word processing package.

Once you have an accurate profile of who is going to use a form or questionnaire you can begin to design it with some confidence.

Why users need forms

The second thing to decide about a new form or questionnaire is why it is needed. Forms can have many purposes, including:

- finding out preferences
- gathering statistics
- requesting additional information
- applying for something.

Once you have found out what the form is going to be used for, the next step is to determine the best format for the user. It is best to do this by creating three or four sample forms and then giving them to a selection of users. Completed forms can be assessed by looking at how accurate the information given is and also by asking the users what they thought of the forms. If the forms have been filled in incorrectly this should not be seen as the fault of the users, but rather the fault of the form. It could mean that a particular question was phrased badly, or that the layout of the form is confusing. If this is the case then you will need to redesign the form. As a general rule, the simpler the form or questionnaire, the better. If users feel intimidated by the form then there is more of a chance that they will not complete it or will make mistakes in doing so. This does not reflect well on the designer of the document and it leads to unnecessary frustration and irritation all round.

CREATING A 'ROAD MAP' FOR THE USERS

At first glance it may seem simple to create forms and questionnaires: just throw together a few questions, add in a suitable number of tick boxes and pepper it with a few boxes for comments for good measure. However, this is a recipe for disaster. The secret of a well-designed form or questionnaire is to create a document that takes the user by the hand and leads them gently but firmly through the entire process of completing all of the necessary sections. In effect this means creating a road map that the user can follow to navigate themselves to their final destinations.

Making it welcoming

It is generally accepted that people do not like filling in forms and they consider it a chore. Therefore, it is the job of the person designing the form to make it look as inviting as possible. A badly designed form will put the recipient in a negative frame of mind from the beginning, making it less likely that they will complete it satisfactorily. Some of the factors that make a form off-putting are:

• tightly packed text

• text that is in all capitals

• narrow margins at the sides, top and bottom

• reply boxes that are too small for the amount of writing required

• large amounts of aggressive colours (such as red) that are tiring on the eye.

Figure 18 shows an example of a form that is intimidating and off-putting.

Encouraging the user

In order to win over the recipient of the form it should be made to look as simple and user-friendly as possible. This can be done in the following ways:

• Using **more informal language**. Instead of saying, 'We require your personal details', try using 'About You' instead.

• Using a **less formal typeface**. Rather than Times Roman use something a bit more rounded like Century Gothic. Experiment to see what effects different typefaces give.

• Using **reply boxes** that are larger than the anticipated amount of text. This means that people will not have to squeeze their handwriting or worry about lining up the form exactly in a typewriter or a computer printer.

COMPLETE THIS FORM AND SEND IT BACK AS SOON AS POSSIBLE. FAILURE TO COMPLY COULD LEAD TO YOUR REQUEST BEING TERMINATED IMMEDIATELY.

SURNAME...

FORENAME(S)...

ADDRESS................................TEL NO...........

REASON FOR REQUEST..

....

SUPPORTING EVIDENCE...

IF THERE IS ANY FURTHER INFORMATION THAT YOU HAVE NOT DISCLOSED THEN THE COMPANY WILL NOT BE HELD RESPONSIBLE FOR ANY ERRORS THAT SUBSEQUENTLY OCCUR. UNFORTUNATELY WE CANNOT ANSWER ANY QUERIES BY TELEPHONE.

Fig. 18. An example of an intimidating form.

- Using **pastel colours** (such as light yellows, greens and blues) for the background of the form. This is not only relaxing on the eye, it also helps to emphasise the reply boxes.

Figure 19 shows an example of a more welcoming form.

Creating navigation points

The design of a good form is more than just getting the information you need down on paper. It is about guiding the recipient through the process of filling in the form. Every effort should be made to ensure this is as painless as possible, or else the form may be filled in incorrectly or not at all.

Lines and arrows

The use of lines and arrows is very useful when designing forms, because it gives the recipient clear guidance about where they should go after they have filled in each bit of information. For instance, if one box has a YES or NO response then there should be arrows that

Preferred Option Loan Form

Please complete this form and return it to us in the prepaid envelope which has been provided. If you have any problems, please do not hesitate to call our FREEPHONE helpline on 0700 12 12 12 and one of our Customer Service Staff will be delighted to help you.

1. About You

First Name(s):

Last Name:

Address:

Post Code:

2. Your Request

Please state your reasons for making this application, including any additional information that may help us process your application more quickly. If necessary, use another piece of paper too.

Thank you for filling in this form

Fig. 19. An example of a welcoming form.

tell the user where to go after each reply. For YES, it may mean that they have to go to a different section from a NO answer and so this should be clearly illustrated. Figure 20 shows how lines and arrows can be used.

Icons
Icons can be used to attract the user's attention and alert them to the fact that a certain piece of information is needed. This is done most frequently with a telephone icon but it can also be used for other items such as personal and financial details. Although icons can be very effective at catching people's attention they should not be over-done or the form may end up looking like a comic book.

Colour coding
Colour coding of forms, or sections of forms, is a popular device when a form is very complicated and has numerous parts to it. Coloured bars along the top or side of the different sections are used to differentiate them so the user can see at a glance where they need to go to find a particular part of the form. The Inland Revenue uses this device with their Tax Return forms. Here, a minefield of information is greatly simplified by the use of colour coding. If you are using this device then make sure that you have a clearly visible box on the front of the form that explains the colour coding system in use.

ENSURING YOUR DOCUMENTS ARE EFFECTIVE

A good form is one that is effective and does its job well, *ie* it obtains the information that it is meant to. Part of this process is making sure that the design is as user-friendly as possible. In addition to this, it is important that the information is completed in such a way that it is a simple task to process the data.

Filling it in
Even the best looking form in the world could be ineffective if the recipient has problems when filling it in. These problems could arise for a number of reasons:

• The user is unsure *where* to put the information.

• The user does not know *how* to enter the information, *eg* by pen, by hand or by typewriter.

• The user does not know how to get the form *back* to the sender.

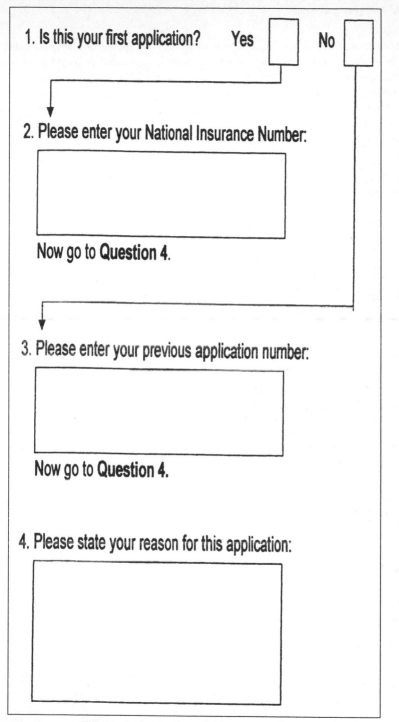

1. Is this your first application?   Yes [ ]   No [ ]

2. Please enter your National Insurance Number:

[   ]

Now go to **Question 4**.

3. Please enter your previous application number:

[   ]

Now go to **Question 4**.

4. Please state your reason for this application:

[   ]

Fig. 20. Using lines and arrows on a form.

Before they are used in a real life situation forms should be road-tested. One way to do this is to give them to people in your organisation and ask them to act as guinea pigs by filling in the form. Do not give them any tips or advice, because it is important that they have the same conditions as the real recipients will have. Once you get the test forms back, analyse them for effectiveness and accuracy. Discuss any problem areas with your colleagues to see why they arose. If necessary, make amendments to the form as a result of this exercise.

If forms are going to be completed under unusual circumstances (such as traffic wardens filling in forms outside and in the dark) it is essential that the testing of the forms takes place under the same conditions. This is because there are sometimes external factors, such as the glare from street lights, which can have an adverse effect on the clarity of the form. Never make any presumptions when you are testing forms; always check them out in the same conditions in which they will be used.

Processing

In addition to ensuring that it is as easy as possible for the users to fill a form in properly there is one more hurdle to overcome: how the information is processed once it has been received back at the point of origination. This can be done in a variety of ways:

- Human processing – people reading the form and then entering the data onto a computer.

- Photocopying – sometimes the information has to be duplicated for official purposes.

- Processing by an Optical Character Recognition (OCR) scanner – this is a machine that acts like an electronic eye that reads the information from the form and then feeds it directly into a computer.

Each of the above has its own drawbacks. The human element relies on the person processing the data being able to read it in the first place. This means that handwriting may not be the best method to convey the information. The standard and quality of handwriting is so varied that it can be very time-consuming and difficult to try and decipher numerous forms that have been filled in by hand. If forms are going to be photocopied then the writing will have to be dark enough for the machine to pick it up. Again this makes handwriting problematic and pencil or coloured inks can also cause difficulties. For an OCR the data has to be typed or produced by a computer printer and it has to be placed in specified areas. This is because the OCR is only programmed to read certain areas on the page and so accuracy of placement is all important.

If there are specific requirements for the processing of the data then this should be clearly stated at the beginning of the form. Comments such as, 'Please complete in black ink', or, 'Please only type in the areas provided', should be displayed prominently, preferably before the user has started to complete the form. You cannot complain about forms not being filled in properly if you do not give the users clear instructions.

MAKING A RESPONSE EASY

Since most people are usually fairly apathetic about completing and returning forms (unless it is for something like a tax rebate) it is a good idea to try and make the process of getting it back to you as painless as possible.

Providing a reply envelope

One of the best ways to ensure that a form is returned is to provide the recipient with an addressed, postage paid envelope in which to return it. This not only saves them from having to buy a stamp but it also means that they do not have to search around on the form to find a return address, which they may then write down incorrectly. Although this can be a costly option you should consider it if you are serious about getting the form back.

Creating a folding form

Some forms are designed so that they can be folded in on themselves and returned using the pre-printed address on the back. Although this can be a little fiddly for the user, it does away with the need for an envelope. Voter registration forms and census forms are often designed in this way – people only have to check the information on them and then fold up the form and post it.

Using electronic forms

With the current advances in computer technology, and greater use of the Internet, it is almost certain that a great deal more form filling is going to be done on-line in the near future. Some organisations, such as banks and insurance companies, already offer Internet services to their customers and this is a rapidly expanding area for consumers. As far as the completion of forms is concerned this is perhaps the easiest medium on offer. The user only has to fill in a few boxes on screen, press a button and their data is automatically sent down the information superhighway.

The electronic transmission of data depends on people having access to the technology in the first place – and also being convinced that this is a secure method of sending information. But as both of these issues are being addressed it is possible that, in time, paper forms could become largely a thing of the past.

SUMMARY

1. Forms are not easy to control. They can, and do, spring up from all corners of an organisation. This makes it very difficult to create a definitive list of all the forms in circulation. Internal forms tend to be harder to keep track of than external ones.

2. The most important person is the user of a form. The user should be consulted at every stage of planning, designing and producing a form.

3. Without forms the business world would grind to a halt. It is therefore a good idea to make them as user-friendly and professional as possible.

ACTION POINTS

1. Produce a robust procedure for generating new forms and revising existing ones.

2. Use different device to make forms look as appealing as possible, *ie* icons, arrows, colour coding and boxes.

3. Always test forms under the same conditions as they are going to be used in.

4. Before you issue a form to the users, ask a selection of people to test the prototype. It is better to find out any problems at this stage rather than when it is 'live'.

5. Make sure you know how forms are going to be processed, and design them with this in mind.

8

Preparing Promotional Material

A vital part of any business is getting people to buy your goods or services and alerting the public when you are trying to do something noteworthy or important. It is all about getting noticed and promoting your product. This can be done in a number of ways:

- Advertising on television, radio, and the press or on dedicated advertising sites such as billboards or bus shelters.

- Sending promotional material directly to your customers or potential customers.

- Issuing press releases to newspapers, magazines and PR companies.

While all of these methods require a different approach they have one thing in common: they are trying to get your business noticed. This means that there has to be an immediate impact and so the style of writing and presentation has to be much more dynamic and direct than other forms of business writing. When you are creating promotional material you may only have a few seconds to persuade the reader to continue. If you fail to do this they will disregard your efforts and move on to something else.

BEING CREATIVE

Design
Since you will have a very short time to get your message across when you are writing promotional material you will need to be more creative in both your use of language and the design of your work. It is also a good idea to employ a little bit of lateral thinking when you are considering the format of your material. Try to look beyond the conventional ideas of standard posters and leaflets. Some of the most effective promotional material comes in an unusual or stimulating format. Consider some of the following:

- Advertisements on **buses** that incorporate the side or the back of the bus into the design of the material. For instance, part of the advertisement may be designed to give the impression of people sitting on the bus.

- Material on the top of **cars or taxis**, so that they can be seen from above.

- Messages on **hot-air balloons** or airships. This is becoming more common but it is always guaranteed to get noticed.

- Promotional material that is incorporated into a **novel design**, *eg* a box of chocolates that opens out to reveal the message, or a CD promoting certain information, or a letter that folds out to create another shape.

When you are thinking of ideas for a new format for promotional material you should keep your target audience in mind and do not get too carried away. If you are targeting a student audience then you may be able to get away with a more *risqué* design than if you are sending items to a predominantly church-going group.

Deploying the personal touch

One of the secrets of successful promotional material is making the reader feel like an individual and that they are a little bit special. This, of course, is an illusion because one piece of direct advertising can be sent to tens of thousands of people. However, it is an effective ploy because we all like to be treated as if we are unique and not just one of the crowd. This personal touch can be achieved in a number of ways:

- Direct mailings that have the recipient's address seemingly hand-written. Although this is really printed, it is intended to give a more personal touch, as if someone has sat down and written each address individually.

- An exotic sounding name for the person who is sending the material, such as Tom Champagne who signs items from Readers Digest. This injects a feeling of excitement and makes the reader feel that they are part of a glamorous promotion.

- Using phrases such as, 'as a valued customer' and 'since we appreciate your business so much', which makes the reader feel as if they are more than just a number on a database.

Whenever you are planning promotional material bear in mind that people will all be reading it as individuals and not as a block of several thousands.

USING LANGUAGE EFFECTIVELY

Headlines

Good headlines are essential in promotional material because these are the first thing that people see. If they do not do their job properly then they may be the only thing people see. The headline has two vital functions:

1. To give the reader a general idea of what is on offer.
2. To arouse their interest enough for them to read on.

It is allowable for headlines in promotional material to be produced all in caps, but only sparingly. Headlines in caps can have a dramatic effect in this medium as long as it is used as a deliberate design feature.

Hooking the reader

Since the idea of the headline is to hook the reader it does not need to go into detail about the product on offer or the company – this can be done in the body of the document. So, if you are promoting a new car that has dramatic fuel economy a headline saying GET THERE FOR LESS would be more effective than saying THE NEW SAHARA USES 12 LITRES LESS THAN THE AVERAGE FAMILY SALOON OVER 100 MILES. While the second headline may be factually correct it is too dry to capture the reader in the first instance. This is useful information but it should be included elsewhere. The first headline conveys an immediate benefit and encourages the reader to continue to see how this can be achieved.

Giving details

In some cases it is a good idea to include specific information in a headline and there are times when the headline makes up all of the promotional material. This is often the case when people are going to be passing quickly, such as in a car or on a train. In this instance it is important to convey as much information as quickly as possible. Some examples of this are:

* 20% OFF EVERYTHING UNTIL 10 JANUARY

- PHONE 0432 1212 FOR A 4.3% LOAN
- SEE FAMILY TIES ON CHANNEL SIX AT 9PM TONIGHT

If the headline does not 'hook' the reader or give them important information then it is doomed to failure.

Choosing the right words

For promotional material to work well then the reader has to feel that there is something in it for them. The first way to achieve this is through your choice of words. The golden rule here is to choose words that will make the reader feel good about him/herself or that they are being offered a genuinely good deal. Words should be short, punchy, upbeat and generate a feeling of excitement or anticipation. Some of the most popular are:

- free
- save
- cheap
- guaranteed
- offer
- safe
- valued
- special
- improve
- pleased
- delighted.

Using some of these could produce a piece of copy that reads, 'As one of our most valued customers we are delighted to offer you a special introductory rate of 2.7 per cent'. This not only makes the recipient feel important, it also makes them believe that they are getting a deal tailored specifically for them.

Words and phrases in promotional material are prone to shifts of fashion just like everything else. A good way to keep up with this is to save the endless stream of leaflets and booklets that come through your door and study them for their use of words and language. At least this way the junk mail is being put to good use!

Sentences and paragraphs

If ever there is a time to cut out long sentences and paragraphs, it is in writing promotional material. Sentences should be short and punchy, including plenty of positive words and phrases and information about how the customer will benefit from the product. Do not go into background detail about the company itself – customers will want to know what is in it for them. In promotional material it is perfectly acceptable to use contractions (YOU'LL BE AMAZED AT THE LOW PRICES), one word sentences (FREE) and sentences beginning with 'and' (AND THAT MEANS MORE MONEY FOR YOU).

Paragraphs should also be short, preferably no more than four or five lines. Readers do not like being confronted by large blocks of text at the best of times and this is doubly true when it is something that they do not have to read at all. You have to make them want to read it by making it look as attractive as possible. Use bold type to emphasise important words and phrases and insert bulleted and numbered lists to break up the text and create areas of white space.

PRODUCING EYE-CATCHING LAYOUTS

Even if you have the best product in the world and the most effective copy for promotional material it could all fall flat if this material is not presented properly. This involves making sure that all of the elements of your material (headlines, body copy and illustrations) are laid out in as effective a way as possible.

Using illustrations

Without a doubt illustrations are the most eye-catching part of any promotional material. A leaflet with a photograph of an adorable puppy will gain a much better response than one with just plain text. The most effective illustrations are photographs that show action or people, or both. People like looking at other people and they also like seeing a product being used.

If you are able to use illustrations then it is important not to waste the opportunity. There is little point in going to a lot of trouble and expense to get illustrations if you then misuse them. Some of the ways to avoid this are:

- Use **photographs** if at all possible. Paintings, drawings and cartoons can be effective but nothing beats the impact of a good photograph. Graphs and charts can be used to demonstrate comparisons or illustrate financial details.

- Use a **professional photographer** to take your photographs. They will know the tricks of the trade (such as getting people to look into the page rather than away from it) and it is well worth the additional expense.

- Keep your illustrations as **big** as possible. Having gone to the trouble of getting them you want to ensure that they have a significant impact. This does not mean that you have to sacrifice headlines or body copy but it is worth bearing in mind that some promotional material has little or no text at all.

- Be wary of images that may give offence or seem to be biased against certain groups or minorities.

GETTING A RESPONSE

The true measure of the success of a promotional item is whether it does its job and gets a response or not. Human nature being what it is, it is best not to leave this to chance – everything possible should be done to encourage the reader to respond to your efforts.

Generate a feeling of urgency
One way to get people to respond is to instil a sense of urgency into the recipient: if they do not reply quickly then they may miss out on a bargain or a special offer. The most common way of doing this is to include a headline that suggests that the customer has to act immediately, or else lose out. Examples of this are:

- BUY NOW!
- OFFER ENDS ON MONDAY
- ONLY TWO LEFT
- FINAL REDUCTIONS THIS WEEKEND

Making it easy to respond

Offering an incentive
One of the best ways of achieving a response is to offer something in return. This usually takes the form of, 'Accept this offer and you will be entitled to a free calculator'. This is effective because the respondent feels as if they are getting something in addition to the original offer. We all like to think that we are getting something for nothing, although in reality this is very seldom the case in the world of promotional material.

Offering a sample or a trial
If people are unsure about whether to take up an offer or not then one way to help persuade them is to offer them a sample or a free

trial. This way they are more likely to respond, safe in the knowledge that they are not actually committing themselves to anything. If you are offering a sample or a trial it is important to stress the customer is not obliged to buy the whole product. This can be done as follows: 'Free 14-day trial of our new stomach toner. If you are not convinced then return it before the end of the trial period. No fuss. No questions asked.'

Using a reply coupon
Coupons are a good way to elicit a reply, as long as they are easy for the customer to detach, fill in and send away. Make sure that they are easily accessible – at the bottom of the page rather than in the middle – and that it is obvious what should be done with them, *ie* cut out, folded, glued or torn down a perforated line. Include as much information as possible on the coupon, so that the customer has to write as little as possible. The return name and address should be clearly printed as should a sentence along the lines of, 'Yes, I would like to accept your introductory offer and enclose a cheque for £5.95'. There should also be enough room for the sender to write in their name and address: there is nothing more off-putting than trying to squeeze your details into a tiny space at the bottom of a page.

CREATING PRESS RELEASES

There is one type of promotional material that is different from standard advertising items: press releases. These are short (usually no more than one page) factual documents that alert the press about an event, such as National Prune Week, a photo shoot featuring a celebrity or a piece of important information. Of course, importance is in the eye of the sender and newspapers, magazines and television and radio newsrooms receive hundreds of press releases every week, each one proclaiming to represent something that simply must appear in the media. Essentially, press releases are all about self-promotion and in order to beat off the competition they need to be carefully thought out and effectively produced.

Getting the words right
Newspaper and television journalists are busy people and they have little time for irrelevant, vague or pretentious press releases. Their practised eye will be able to spot an unprofessional press release from more than 20 paces and after that they will not give it a second glance. Because you are dealing with professional journalists you will have

to think and write like a journalist in order to get their attention. (Even this may not ensure that your item is published but that could come down to reasons such as space, suitability or timing. The important thing is to get your press release read.) The first step in this is to follow the five Ws of journalism:

- **Who** – who is the item about? Are they a celebrity, either locally or nationally? Are they an expert in their field?

- **What** – describe the facts of the item. Has something particularly good, bad or unusual happened?

- **Where** – detail where the event has taken place or, if it is still to take place, give information about this and how the press can get there.

- **When** – give precise dates and times. This is particularly important if you are arranging something like a photo-shoot, as it is essential that everyone is there at the right time.

- **Why** – what makes this item more newsworthy than one of your competitors.

Once you have the five Ws, you should present them in a clear, simple and, above all, concise style. If you are successful in conveying the five Ws then the journalist reading it will be able to make a quick decision about whether to follow up the item. If you go on too much then they may become bored or irritated and move on to the next press release. Give them the essential facts and then let them take it from there.

Making it look good

The layout of a press release is not about extravagant designs and expensive images: it is about giving the reader the information they need as quickly as possible. By all means, make it look as professional as you can but do not go over the top as this may detract from the message in the press release itself.

A good press release should be headed up in a similar way to a memo and include at least some of the following items before you start your body copy:

- name of the sender

- the organisation it comes from

- contact name, telephone number, fax number and email

- date

- an embargo time, if applicable, *ie* the time before which the information should not be broadcast

- a brief description of the subject matter.

All of this should be in a clear, reasonably sized typeface so that the reader can see at a glance whether it is worth reading any further. Figure 21 shows the layout for a press release.

DDC: Developing for the future

Press Release

FROM: Digital Development Company
TO: All national news editors
Contact: Caroline Whately
Telephone: 0334 98693
Fax: 0334 98694
Email: Caroline@Digital.co.uk
Release time: Immediate

Subject: New Chip for faster Internet Access

Digital Development Company is delighted to announce a major breakthrough in the battle of supremacy of the Internet. Trials have just been successfully concluded of a revolutionary microchip, called iChip, which is guaranteed to decrease downloading time on the Net by 50%.

The iChip combines the latest micro-technology with a dynamic design system that is equally at home downloading text, graphics, video clips or sound. In trial it proved to be 100% effective.

A demonstration of the iChip will take place on Wednesday 2 October 1999 at our headquarters in Birmingham: 1–10 Digital House, New Street, Birmingham. There will also be a chance to take photographs. For further information please contact Caroline Whately at any of the above numbers.

Fig. 21. An example of a press release.

SUMMARY

1. Promotional material is not quite the same as other forms of business writing. Since it involves sending out unsolicited material the style can be more dynamic and innovative. It is an area where imagination is more important than following convention.

2. As long as you keep within the boundaries of decency and good taste, then you can let your creative side run wild. Ground-breaking promotional material is appearing all the time.

3. Promotional material has to make an immediate impact. You will only have a few seconds, or a few words, to catch the reader's attention. This can be done by design or use of language, but either way it has to be dramatic.

ACTION POINTS

1. Collect as many items of promotional material as you can. Analyse them to see if they are effective and if so why.

2. Create a list of words and phrases that appear most frequently in promotional material.

3. Pick an imaginary product and create half a dozen different types of promotional material to advertise it.

4. Think of ways to create innovative designs for promotional material. Look at everyday objects and see if they could be incorporated into your design.

5. Compile a list of illustrations to use for promotional material. This should include the use of a professional photographer.

9

Presenting Financial Information

If you mention financial data to people who are more familiar with dealing with words then their eyes will probably glaze over and they will break out in a cold sweat. In general, people who produce written communications feel uneasy when they have to confront financial information or statistics. But it is an integral part of the business world, ranging from sales figures to absence statistics, so it is best to take the bull by the horns and accept that sooner rather than later you are going to have to produce documents that include at least some financial information.

CHOOSING THE RELEVANT DATA

Deciding what is important

By its very nature, financial information is frequently complicated and in-depth. This is invariably because it is produced by accountants and statisticians who view the world slightly differently from the people who have to present the information in a digestible form to an unsuspecting public. The statisticians will argue that as long as the information is in a document then they have done their job. While this is true, it then falls to someone else to decide on the best way to present this information. This happens frequently in the business world, where the public is given only a small part of the overall information that has been provided. For example:

- The monthly inflation and unemployment figures: the headlines that appear in newspapers and on television usually only refer to the main figures. But this is just the tip of the iceberg: there is a wealth of other data that is mainly of interest to economists and political commentators.

- Company results and profits: although most companies publish an annual report that contains the full accounts for the year, what most of us see is the overall profit or loss figure and the annual turnover.

- Interest rates and mortgage rates.

In each of the above examples the organisation with the data decides which figures are the most important for the relevant audience and publishes them accordingly. This way the attention is focused on one part of the data rather than subjecting the recipient to swathes of statistics and figures.

ORGANISING YOUR DATA

Using all of your sources

When errors occur with numerical data it is not always because of mistakes in the available information: it is sometimes because of what has been left out. When you are compiling data, such as the monthly sales figures, it is essential that you make sure that you have every available item of information. If you do not, then you will end up with figures that are inaccurate and misleading.

Begin by identifying the areas from which you want information. Then contact the relevant people and tell them exactly what you want. Accuracy is very important so there is no point in asking for, 'sales figures for January', when what you really want is, 'sales figures of product X for January'. Make sure that you have a record of what you ask for and let people know if this will be a one-off request or a recurring one.

Being logical

Once you have gathered all the information you need you should organise it so you have an in-depth understanding of the data and how it relates to what you are going to produce.

Begin by reading through all of the data and putting aside anything that is irrelevant to the project in hand. (This does not mean you have to dispose of it completely, as it may be useful for something or someone else.) Then arrange the information into relevant groups. This may be 'income' and 'expenditure' or sales figures for specific areas. Make sure that you are clear about what you are doing and why you are doing it: if you feel you are getting lost then stop and go back a step.

Once you are confident with the information that you want to work with you can begin to process it. You may want to do this on a computer or work with a hard copy. The best way is the one with which you feel most comfortable.

USING SPREADSHEETS

Defining spreadsheets

Spreadsheets are one of the staples of financial information. Due to powerful computer software packages spreadsheets are now available that can number-crunch even the most complicated financial or scientific material. This has led to even the most number-shy employee being able to produce pages and pages of impressive looking facts and figures. However, depending on how these are used, this can have a positive or a negative effect.

Compiling databases

One of the main uses for spreadsheet programs is to create databases. These are basically large lists of information that are held on computers instead of in paper files. Databases can include a wide variety of information:

- consumer shopping habits
- employee records
- book titles in libraries
- banking details
- stock lists
- sporting fixtures
- customer clients.

Once a database has been created it can be manipulated in a number of ways: it can be sorted under a variety of criteria, calculations can be made and trends can be identified. However, databases are not usually published in external documents. The reasons for this are twofold:

1. They are invariably so large that it would be impractical to produce them in a hard copy. Also, they are easier to work with when they are on a computer.

2. There are various implications under the Data Protection Act 1984, which governs the use and disclosure of electronically held information.

Presenting spreadsheets

Graphical presentation

When you have to publish information from spreadsheets the most important factor is the old adage from the writing world: 'know your audience'. This means that if you are presenting it to the board of directors you can include fairly detailed and complex information, but if you are presenting it to the workforce in general then a more broadbrush approach is required.

One of the best ways to present data from spreadsheets is with graphs and charts. These range from a straightforward pie chart to more complicated integrated graphs. Charts and graphs are discussed in more detail in the following section but remember:

- general audience – keep it simple
- expert audience – provide in-depth information.

Textual presentation

If you want to present your spreadsheet information in a straightforward fashion then this can be done in two ways:

1. For senior managers and the decision-makers in your organisation you can print spreadsheets in their entirety. This way they not only see the final result but also the figures that went into creating it. This can be useful because it can help to identify patterns and trends.

2. For employees in general, who are more interested in the headline figures than trawling through pages and pages of statistics, the most relevant data could be incorporated into another medium. For instance, monthly sales figures could be included in an article in the organisation's newsletter along the lines of, 'In July the sales of semi-conductor cables was 25,000, up 12 per cent on the previous month'. This conveys the necessary information without overloading people with the detail.

INCORPORATING GRAPHS AND CHARTS

The most visually pleasing way of presenting numerical information is in the form of graphs and charts. Modern computer programs produce these in a variety of shapes and sizes, all at the touch of a button. However, in order to use them to their maximum effect it is useful to know the different situations that best suit each format.

Working with graphs

In general, graphs are at their most effective when you want to demonstrate a trend over a period of weeks or months. This is per-

haps most commonly seen when we are shown on television the fluc-
tuations in interest rates. Graphs are also valuable if you want to draw
a comparison between two sets of figures. Again, this is often seen
on television when analysts are comparing current unemployment figures with those of twelve months earlier.

The secret of a good graph is to include a limited amount of information and make sure there is an adequate description to tell the
reader what it is all about. This should include:

- a main title

- a legend which defines each line on the graph

- a value for the x-axis and the y-axis (such as '£s' or '1,000s')

- any notes or additional information that may be of use to the
  reader.

Be careful not to make your graph look too cluttered, or else the
reader will become confused. If you have six sets of figures to com-
pare it is better to have either three graphs with two lines each or two
graphs with three each, rather than one complicated graph with six
lines. Some examples of basic graph formats are shown in Figure 22.

Working with charts

Charts come in an equally diverse range of styles as graphs and they
are best at showing the proportional relationship between sets of figures. For instance, a bar chart could show at a glance the propor-
tionate increase in monthly sales figures and a pie chart could
demonstrate the percentage of working days lost during a specific
period. As with graphs, charts are most effective when they are dealing with up to six figures: any more and the end product can look
confusing and some of the data becomes too small to be presented
effectively. Some examples of charts are shown in Figure 23.

GIVING IT MEANING

Knowing what it is yourself

Numerical data is frequently complicated and technical. This problem becomes more acute when you are trying to analyse and explain
the results to other people. However, in order to do this as confi-
dently as possible it is important that you fully understand the data
yourself. This may seem like an obvious point but if you have been

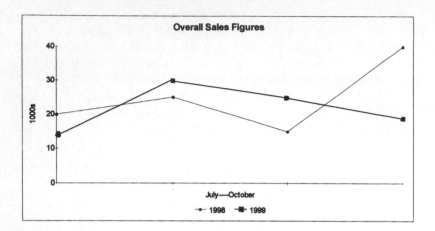

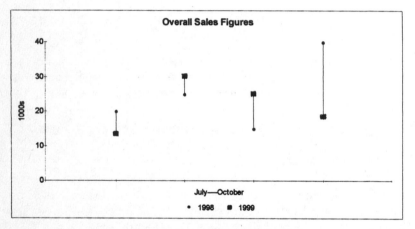

Fig. 22. An example of graphs.

working closely with the information then you may have absorbed certain parts of it more than others and placed your own interpretation on the figures. Before you start trying to explain it to other people, go over each part of it yourself and make sure that you know what each individual chart and graph means and also how they relate to each other. As a final check, it is a good idea to get a colleague to look at the information and ask you questions about it. It is always worth getting a fresh view from someone who does not know the information as well as you do. They could point out something apparently obvious that you have overlooked.

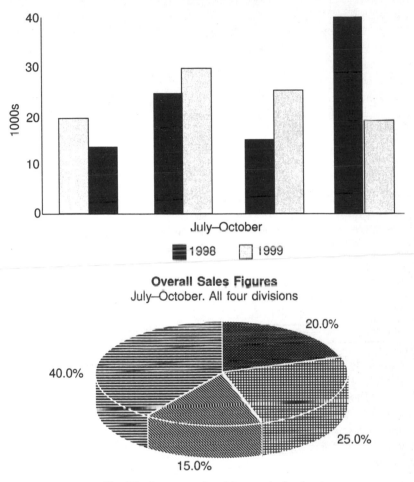

Fig. 23. An example of bar and pie charts

Applying the lowest common denominator

Knowing your audience is essential when you are presenting numerical information. If the audience is experienced and knowledgeable about the topic then you will not need to provide much background information and explanatory notes. But if you are dealing with a group of people who are not familiar with the information you are presenting then you will have to look at it from their viewpoint. This means thinking about the person who has the least knowledge about the topic and then acting accordingly. In order to find this out you should ask yourself the following questions:

- Is the information going to be seen by the **general public**? If so you will have to presume that they have a low level of knowledge. Therefore you will have to explain the situation from the beginning. Just because something is obvious to you it does not mean that it makes the same amount of sense to everyone else.

- Is the information being presented to **external organisations**? If so, what is their prior knowledge of the topic? This will probably be more than the general public but you should not make the mistake of becoming too insular and thinking that other businesses share exactly the same knowledge as your own.

- Is the information being made available throughout **your own organisation**? This makes it easier to presume a certain level of knowledge but it is worth remembering that people in your finance division may have differing expertise from your sales staff.

- Is the information for a **specific group** within your organisation, such as an executive board or group? If so, then you will be able to target the information more specifically as it will be easier to determine their areas of interest and levels of knowledge.

Presenting it well

Even the most dramatic numerical information can be wasted or become ineffective if it is not presented in a digestible format for the audience. The style of presentation is essential in this respect because conveying the data to the target audience is the whole point of the exercise. The first thing to ascertain is how the information is going to be presented:

- Is it for an on-screen or projected presentation?
- Will it be incorporated into the body of a document?
- Will it appear as a separate annex or appendix?

Each of these will require a slightly different approach to the presentation of the data.

On-screen or projected

The most common form of projected presentation is one where computer generated slides are projected onto a screen via an overhead projector (OHP) or a laptop computer. The audience can then view enlarged versions of the slides. When this form of presentation is used for numerical data a few common-sense rules should be followed:

- Make sure there is a **good contrast** between the background colour and the colour in which the information is displayed. If the background is dark then make the foreground light and vice versa. If in doubt, black on white is a perfectly acceptable colour scheme, if a little cheerless.

- Use **more slides** rather than cramming in information. Since modern presentational materials can ensure a virtually seamless transition from one slide to another it is best to use one slide for each item of information.

- The numerical information should be produced **as large as possible**. It is no use having an intricate chart or graph if it is too small to be seen properly.

- Always **run through** your presentation before you unleash it on your unsuspecting public. This is useful for your own benefit, so that you can rehearse what you are going to say, and it also alerts you to any problems.

Incorporated in the body of the document
If your numerical information appears in the body of the document then you should make sure that it is clearly referred to in the text and also that it has an adequate caption attached to it, such as 'Figure 14. Monthly sales results from the north-east division'. Tables, charts and graphs can be incorporated into the text or they can be placed on a separate page next to it. Either way they should be clear and unambiguous.

Separate appendix
Numerical information that is placed in an appendix or an annex is usually for the benefit of people who are particularly interested in it, such as yearly accounts that invariably appear at the end of a company's annual report. Since this is a more specialised area it is reasonable to include more information per page than you might do otherwise. Since the readers will be familiar with this type of information, and the format, they will be able to assimilate it more quickly. However, every effort should still be made to make it look as appealing as possible.

SUMMARY

1. You may well have to work with charts and graphs even though you have nothing to do with the financial side of the organisation. You could find yourself doing a presentation that has this kind of information included in it or you may need to write a proposal that requires figures to back up some of your arguments. Always be prepared for the unexpected in the world of business writing.

2. It is best to get financial data checked by the experts. Even if you think it is perfectly clear, it is always a good idea to get a second opinion from the financial people. This is because there may be some hidden numerical factor that you have overlooked or did not know about.

3. Numerical information does not have to be complicated and intimidating. As with other forms of business writing, clarity is the best approach to take. Numerical information is just like anything else; if it is not clear then it will be ignored.

ACTION POINTS

1. Become as familiar as you can with spreadsheets and databases, even if you do not usually use them in your own work.

2. Experiment with different styles of charts to see which ones you feel are the clearest and the most visually effective.

3. Find out who is going to be reading the numerical information and then create it for their level.

4. Always give a textual explanation of any numerical information. Not everyone is an accountant or a financial whizz-kid.

5. Do not be afraid to seek advice about presenting numerical data. It can be a difficult area and no one should criticise you for asking for help.

10

Dealing with Email

If there is one medium that has contributed to an explosion in business correspondence in recent years, both internally and externally, then it is email. Email allows the users to send messages and attachments from one computer to any number of others connected to the network. The advantages of email are that it can be delivered instantly, unlike hand delivered mail (or snail mail as computer devotees disparagingly call it), and it can reach a large audience at the touch of a button. On the downside, it is frequently used unnecessarily. Also, it is a myth that email reduces the paper mountain in the business world: in fact the reverse is true since most people print out their email, 'just to be on the safe side'.

THE BASIC FUNCTIONS

There are numerous different email systems on the market but they all perform the same basic task. This involves composing, sending and receiving messages and this can be done through a selection of methods.

Composing email

Email can be composed for either internal or external customers who either have access to your internal computer network or have a modem and related software through which they can access messages. When you create your email you can either enter the email address of the recipient or choose names from an Address Book. This is a list of names and email addresses that can be selected without the hassle of typing in the whole address from scratch. These lists can be easily edited.

Setting up email groups

If you regularly send messages to the same group of people then you can set them up as a **group** in your email address book. For instance, if you send a weekly report to the same group of managers then you can group them altogether under one heading, *eg* WeekReport. This way, you only have to select the group for the relevant people to be included in the correspondence. One word of warning: if you then decide to send different information to the group you should check carefully to make sure that the data really is appropriate for all of them. Groups can be created for a variety of correspondence but you should always be prepared to amend and edit the personnel in them.

Sending email

When you want to send an email you usually have the choice of sending it immediately or saving it to send later. If speed is of the essence then the first option is the one to take but there are a number of advantages to saving and sending later. These include:

- **Price**. Since external emails are transmitted via telephone lines it can be cheaper to send them when the telephone charges are low, *ie* in the evenings and at weekends.

- **Availability**. If you know someone is away on holiday you may want to wait until they return to email them. This is for the simple reason that circumstances may change and you do not want to send them something that may seem out-of-date. Also, there is nothing worse then coming back from holiday to discover that you have dozens of emails waiting for you.

- **Reflection**. With all forms of business writing it is a good idea to have a 'cooling-off' period between finishing something and sending it. This is certainly true with email, where items can be written and sent in the heat of the moment.

UNDERSTANDING THE TECHNICAL SIDE

Although it is not essential to know about all the technical details of email it is a good idea to have a basic knowledge of how the system works. This will allow you to use it more effectively and productively.

Servers

In simple terms, email works by allowing a network of computers to communicate with each other. This can be done on an office, national or international basis. What links the computers is a **server**, which is basically another computer which, among other things, receives and routes email messages. (This is usually done in conjunction with access to the Internet.) So when an email is sent it goes to the server, which then works out where to send the message on to. This could involve it communicating with other servers, which are in turn connected to the recipient. Servers can operate within local area networks (LANs) or wide area networks (WANs) and, in general, the further the email is sent then the more servers will be involved.

Handling memory and disc space

As with most things involving computers, speed and disc storage space are both important considerations. The speed at which your message can be transmitted relies largely on its length and the quality of the telephone cables along which it is travelling. This is being improved on an almost daily basis and in general a simple text-only email message can usually be delivered within a minute or two of it being sent. Including pictures or diagrams will take longer as it takes more time to transfer this type of information along the telephone lines. Internal email should not take long to deliver unless there is a considerable strain on the internal network.

One factor that will slow down the delivery of email is the number of users trying to connect to a server at the same time. For instance, if everyone in an organisation wanted to send an email at 10am then there may be a bottleneck as the server tries to deal with all of these simultaneous requests. The best thing to do is to wait until you know the network will be quieter. Your network adviser in the IT department should be able to tell you when the light usage periods are in the day.

UNDERSTANDING CONVENTIONS AND ETIQUETTE

Although there are no hard and fast rules for what you should and should not do when writing and sending emails, a certain amount of common sense should be applied. If not, there is the danger of people being swamped with electronic messages.

Replying and forwarding

Two of the most frequently used functions of email are **Reply** and **Forward**. These allow the recipient of an email to reply directly to the sender without having to first enter the address, or to forward the message to other interested parties. This allows for quick and easy communication but it can have its drawbacks if it is not used with some thought.

Using the Reply function

When using the **Reply** function you should be mindful of the message that has been sent to you in the first place, since this is also returned to the sender along with your reply. So if a two-page long email is sent to you that only requires a reply along the lines of, 'Yes I will be able to attend the meeting', then it may be more practical to send your own message to that effect. This will not only cut down on the length of emails being sent backwards and forwards but it also adds a more personal touch by showing you have made the effort to send an individual reply.

Using the Reply All function

Another area that needs to be treated carefully is the **Reply All** function. This enables a recipient, who has been sent an email as part of a larger group, automatically to send a reply to all of the other members of the group. While this can be useful if you want to reply to several people quickly, you can run the risk of sending unnecessary messages. If you really want to contact only two or three of the people in the group then it is a waste of resources and time to send it to everybody on a particular list. When you are replying to email it is worth thinking about who you really want to contact and then send your messages accordingly.

Copying emails

The **Copy** function (cc) allows the sender to copy the message to people who do not necessarily need to act on the information but who may find it useful to know what is going on. When emails are copied to other people there is the danger that the original recipient will feel as if they are not fully trusted. This may or may not be the case and when emails are copied it is important that the seniority of all those involved is taken into consideration. Generally, copying emails to a higher grade is viewed with a certain degree of suspicion.

Urgent and return receipts

By their very nature emails are a way of communicating with people quickly. Because of this, people often view their emails as vitally important and expect a response within minutes of them being sent. To achieve this an 'urgent' tag is frequently attached to the document. This appears on the recipient's screen as some form of identifier such as an exclamation mark. While it is true that some emails *are* urgent, the majority of them are not, much as the sender would protest to the contrary. If urgent tags are constantly being attached to non-urgent messages this can have a counter-productive effect: recipients get fed up with receiving what they see as pushy emails and so they put them at the bottom of their list of priorities.

Rather than attach an urgent tag to every email message a more productive method can be to include a return receipt with your correspondence. This informs you when the email was accessed and if no response is forthcoming you can try to generate a reply through a follow-up telephone call, safe in the knowledge that your email has been looked at. This function is only available for internal emails.

Urgent and return receipt tags can usually be added by using the Options function on your email toolbar.

Avoiding 'emoticons'

One of the most common criticisms of email is that it is an unemotional medium that does not allow for any body language or visual clues as to the mood of the writer. Of course this is equally true of letters and memos but the problem seems to be exacerbated by email, as if a computer screen is even more of an impersonal barrier than a piece of paper. One way to try and overcome this is to write in a more informal or relaxed way than you would normally. While this can be effective in some instances, the writer also runs the risk of appearing overly familiar or flippant. The worst case scenario is that the recipient could take your tone entirely the wrong way, thus giving rise to a bout of 'email rage' (see below).

In order to try and solve the problem of characterless and impenetrable emails one computer bright spark with too much time on his or her hands came up with the idea of 'emoticons' or 'smileys'. These are collections of characters that are intended to convey emotions, such as happiness, sadness, irritation *etc*. For instance, an uplifting email could be introduced by the following emoticon – :-). There are hundreds of these emoticons in circulation but unless you are sending an informal email to a close friend it is best to steer clear of them altogether. Business people usually have better things to do than to gaze at cute little email symbols.

COMPOSING MEANINGFUL EMAILS

One of the drawbacks of email is that its instanteity in creation and distribution gives the writer a false sense of bravado. This can lead to carelessness and a lack of professionalism that would not occur in other forms of business correspondence. Just because the format of an email is more informal than a business letter or a memo it does not mean that email should be treated as a lesser form of communication. Indeed, because of the more flexible nature of the medium, extra care is needed when composing email to ensure that the right tone and style are employed for the recipient or recipients. This means that particular attention should be paid to the following areas:

- planning
- composing
- checking.

Planning the text and destination

Before you launch yourself into cyberspace it is important to plan what you are going to say and to whom you are going to say it. To people who sit down at their computers first thing in the morning and dash off half a dozen emails before their first cup of coffee this may seem like an unnecessarily complicated way to go about things. However, for emails to be effective they need to be given the same care and attention as other pieces of business correspondence.

Choosing your destination
Before you start thinking about the text you should work out who needs to see a copy of the email. This is where a little restraint is needed: just because you *can* send an email to someone does it mean that you have to? All too often emails are sent to people because it is technically possible, rather than because they actually need to see it. A good exercise is to imagine you are writing a traditional letter and then work out how many copies you would print out and put into envelopes.

Planning the text
Having defined your audience you can then get on with the task of planning what you are going to say. This should be done in a similar way to writing a business letter or a memo and include the following points:

- A strong **introduction** that is concise and sets out the topics or ideas that you want to include.

- The **body** of the document contains everything that you want to cover. Each point should begin with a separate paragraph and should be as straightforward and simple as possible. Just because something is being written in email does not mean that the clarity of meaning can be compromised.

- The **ending** summarises what you have said in the body of the document and, if relevant, asks for comments or feedback.

Composing your email

Although there is no logical reason for emails to be written in a different style to a business letter or a memo, they invariably are. People facing an email screen often feel that they have a power that does not come with a piece of paper; as if the anonymity of the computer network shields them from the harsh realities of the business world. This often leads to emails that are uncharacteristically bold or even arrogant.

The greeting

The main difference between an email and a letter or a memo is in the opening. The writer does not need to include their own details or those of the recipient because these will be displayed by the relevant computer. All the writer has to do is to select the names of the people the email is to go to, including anyone it is being copied to, enter the subject and then begin writing.

Some people still like to begin emails 'Dear Bill . . .', or even just 'Bill', while others consider that the information displayed at the top of the screen is enough and so just go straight into the text. There is no hard and fast rule for this but generally if you are emailing one person then some form of greeting is polite, while if you are contacting a group of people it is impractical to address them all personally.

The body

The body of an email should be written in the same style as a letter or memo. Do not get carried away with asides or anecdotes and avoid any attempts at humour. The same rules apply here as for any other form of business writing – you may think a certain joke is hilarious but the chances are the humour will be lost on other people.

The ending

As with the greeting, the ending of an email can be ambiguous. The conventions of 'Yours sincerely' and 'Yours faithfully' do not apply and it is more common for an email to end with a phrase such as 'Best wishes' or 'Hope to hear from you soon'. If in doubt you can leave out the ending altogether and just type your name at the bottom of the email.

Checking your emails

Many problems with emails arise when the writer constructs them in haste and then sends them off without giving them a second thought. This is the product of the technology that allows for correspondence to be read only minutes after it has been written. While this has the advantage of speed, it can also lead to documents that have not been checked properly, as writers seem to think that speed of delivery demands an equal speed of writing. Even if this is the case it is vital that emails are checked for accuracy and also overall tone. There is little point in having a brainwave and emailing it to the chief executive if your message is sloppy and error-strewn. A period of calm reflection is always a good idea once an email has been written and before it is sent.

AVOIDING 'EMAIL RAGE'

Defining email rage

First we had 'road rage' as motorists lost their temper with increasing regularity, then it was 'trolley rage' as irate shoppers began taking the law into their own hands, and now 'email rage' is coursing through our computers at work. This occurs when emails are ill conceived or taken the wrong way: after a few minutes of sending messages back and forward a minor disagreement or misunderstanding has been blown up into a major incident.

Combating email rage

The main causes of email rage are the speed with which the system can operate and the ambiguity of some of the messages. Because emails can be delivered in the blink of an eye some people compose their messages with a similar speed and then when it is received the sudden impact of it can result in a flare-up that leaves the computer terminals red-hot.

Think before you send

All types of business correspondence should be left for a period of time before they are despatched and this is doubly true for email. Invariably if you are under stress or annoyed about something this will be translated into your writing. With an email, the message could be with the recipient before you have had time to calm down. This in turn can generate bad feeling with the person who has received the message, and so it goes on.

If you have written an email because you are annoyed or angry it is essential that you leave a period of at least an hour, and preferably two, before you send it. Save it on your system and then forget about it and go away and do something else. When you come back to it you may be horrified at the message you intended to send and thank your lucky stars that you have a chance to amend it. Email composed in anger and sent in haste can be a recipe for disaster.

Making it clear
Even with the best will in the world, your words and phrases can be misconstrued. As a communication medium email seems to exaggerate this problem. Perhaps it is the immediacy of it, or the appearance of it on a computer screen as opposed to a piece of paper. Whatever the reason, it is best to re-read the text before you send your email, just to make sure it is clear and not open to misinterpretation.

If a problem does arise then it is best not to try and resolve it by entering into an extended emailing session. This may only serve to distort the problem further. If in doubt, resort to that old-fashioned method of actually talking to the individual involved, either by telephone or in person.

SUMMARY

1. With the exception of the telephone email is the quickest way to communicate with work colleagues. However, this does depend on the other person being at their computer and actually checking their incoming emails regularly.

2. Emails should be efficient, but because it is easy to copy and forward emails to large numbers of people, the medium is often wasteful and cumbersome. To avoid this users should be more thoughtful about their own approach to email.

3. Email is not always harmless. It can sometimes cause problems by allowing viruses to enter your network from an external source, and sometimes employers can be held responsible if their employees abuse the system by sending offensive or spurious emails.

ACTION POINTS

1. Familiarise yourself with the technical side of email. Although this may not be essential it is useful to know and could come in handy if there are problems with the system.

2. Always think before you email. Emails are often copied to people who do not need them which is a waste of both time and resources.

3. Leave a period of time (at least an hour, if possible, and preferably longer) between writing an email and sending it. This will give you a chance to reread your message and ensure it really says what you want.

4. Never send an email when you are feeling angry or irritated. This is a recipe for disaster and could lead to a mountain of unpleasant electronic correspondence.

5. Compile a set of guidelines for the dos and don'ts of email use. Be precise about what is allowed and what is viewed as unacceptable.

Glossary

Bar chart. A device for presenting numerical data, where the information is converted into columns on a chart.

Brainstorming. A method for generating ideas, where everything thought of is written down and then edited.

Brief. A set of instructions from which a report or a proposal can be written.

cc. Used to indicate that a document has been copied to another person or persons. (Stands for 'carbon copies' or 'copies'.)

Clip Art. Graphical images that come pre-loaded onto most computers these days. Should be used sparingly.

Copy. The name given to text for an article in a newspaper or a newsletter. Can also apply to the text for promotional material.

Database. Computer software that is capable of storing large amounts of data – such as a list of client addresses.

Email. Electronic mail that is sent via computer systems and networks. An increasingly common method of communication in the business world.

Email rage. A condition that is caused by people writing and sending emails in haste, without thinking about what they are really saying.

Emoticons. A collection of symbols that are supposed to inject feelings into email message. Best avoided if possible.

Eyeflow. The way that we read a page of text. We usually start somewhere near the middle, work up to the top left-hand corner and then scan the page in a lazy pattern.

Five Ws. The golden rules to follow in journalism: who, what, when, where, why.

Font. A complete set of type of one size and style, *eg* Courier bold, Courier italic and Courier light.

Formatting. Presenting text so that all the different parts of a document are easily recognised, *eg* headlines of different importance and the body text.

Graph. A device for presenting numerical data, where the information is converted into lines on a chart.

Grid. The method for determining the appearance of a newsletter or a magazine. The shape of the grid is decided at the beginning (usually a one, two or three column grid) and then this is used for all of the pages in the publication.

Hard copy. A paper version of a document, as opposed to one that is on a computer screen.

Icons. Small symbols that can be used to denote items such as telephone numbers.

Internet. The collection of computers, servers and modems around the world that are connected together in order to be able to share information (see World Wide Web).

Layout. The method of incorporating text and illustrations on a page.

Linkback. A device in a newspaper or magazine article that links something at the end of the feature back to the introduction.

Logo. A symbol and/or name that is identified with a particular company. Logos are usually unique to one company.

Masthead. Additional information about a newsletter or magazine, and the company that produces it, that usually appears in the inside of the production. Sometimes used instead of **nameplate**.

Nameplate. The name and title of a newsletter or magazine, as it appears on the front page.

Outline. A shortened version of a business document, from which the full-length version if written. Frequently written in note form.

Pie chart. A device for presenting numerical data, where the information is converted into circular charts.

Point size. The size of text in a document.

Proof-reading. A method for checking text for accuracy and readability.

Return receipt. The method for identifying when someone has opened a particular email.

Server. A piece of computer software that, among other tasks, collects email messages and then sends them on to the recipient.

Signposts. A device in a newsletter or magazine article that alerts the reader to the fact that there is a change in direction or emphasis coming up.

Topic identifier. A line in a letter, after the greeting and before the body of the letter, that tells the recipient what the letter is about.

Typeface. The design of a particular family of characters, *eg* Arial, Baskerville, Times Roman.

World Wide Web (WWW). The collection of information that is displayed on the Internet. This is made up of millions of pages, ranging from the innovative to the appalling.

Further Reading

Writing Business Letters, 2nd edition, Ann Dobson (How To Books).
Mastering Business English, 3rd edition, Michael Bennie (How To Books).
Writing a Report, 4th edition, John Bowden (How To Books).
Designing for Desktop Publishing, Diane Hudson (How To Books, 1998).
How to Publish a Newsletter, 2nd edition, Graham Jones (How To Books).
Collins Gem English Grammar, Ronald G Hardie (HarperCollins, 1990).
English Grammar, An Outline, Rodney Huddleston (Cambridge University Press, 1988).
Teach Yourself English Grammar, B Phythian (Hodder & Stoughton, 1992).
Teach Yourself Correct English, B Phythian (Hodder & Stoughton, 1992).
Mother Tongue, Bill Bryson (Penguin Books, 1991).
Troublesome Words, Bill Bryson (Penguin Books, 1997).
Layout, Design and Typography for the Desktop Publisher, Gerald A Silver (Wm C. Brown, 1991).
Elements of Business Writing, Gary Blake and Robert W Bly (Collier Books US, 1992).
Better Business Writing, Maryann V Piotrowski (Piatkus Books, 1992).

Index

MASTERING BUSINESS ENGLISH
How to sharpen up your communication skills at work

Michael Bennie

Good communication is the key to success in any business. Whether you are trying to sell a product, answer a query or complaint, or persuade colleagues, the way you express yourself is often as important as what you say. With lots of examples, checklists and questionnaires to help you, the newly updated edition of this book will speed you on your way. 'Gives guidance on writing styles for every situation . . . steers the reader through principles and techniques of effective letter-writing and document-planning.' *First Voice.* 'Useful chapters on grammar, punctuation and spelling. Frequent questionnaires and checklists enable the reader to check progress.' *Focus,* Society of Business Teachers. 'Easy to follow . . . Excellent value for money.' *Spoken English.*

208pp. illus. 1 85703 376 0. 4th edition.

UNLOCKING YOUR POTENTIAL
How to master your mind, life and destiny

Peter Marshall

Even the smartest individuals will not fulfil their potential on intellect alone; first they must free themselves from their own limiting expectations. If you really want to become master of your own life you will need to remove the barriers to success. This book will show you how to do it. It will introduce you to objective techniques for overcoming the limiting effects of the past: conditioning, misguided or obsolete teachings, repressed conflicts and the expectations imposed on us by others. Peter Marshall is a research psychologist, who specialises in mind and memory, and is a member of the Applied Psychology Research Group of the University of London. He is author of *How to Study and Learn* and *Research Methods* in this series.

104pp. 1 85703 252 7.

MANAGING MEETINGS
How to prepare, how to take part and how to follow up

Ann Dobson

This book is divided into two parts: the first covers the key skills of communicating effectively, motivating and persuading, problem-solving, decision-making, body language, and dealing with troublemakers. Part 2 deals with the practical steps of holding a meeting and following up. Case studies, self-assessment material and checklists complete the simple, yet effective approach.

124pp. illus. 1 85703 222 5.

THRIVING ON STRESS
How to manage pressures and transform your life

Jan Sutton

The pressures of modern life make us susceptible to stress. However not all stress is negative – if managed effectively we can positively thrive on it. Peak performance stress stimulates activity, enhances creativity, and motivates us to live happy and fulfiling lives. Drawing on her experience as a counsellor, stress management and assertiveness trainer, Jan Sutton not only equips you with easily mastered strategies for conquering negative stress, she also offers you a personal development programme for building self-esteem and self-confidence. The book is complete with comprehensive case studies, illustrations, and practical activities. Jan Sutton (Dip CPC) is co-author (with William Stewart) of *Learning to Counsel* in this series.

192pp. illus. 1 85703 238 1.

WRITING BUSINESS LETTERS
How to tackle your day-to-day business correspondence successfully

Ann Dobson

Intended for absolute beginners, this book uses fictional characters in a typical business setting to contrast the right and wrong ways to go about things. Taking nothing for granted, the book shows: how to plan a letter, how to write and present it, how to deal with requests, how to write and answer complaints, standard letters, personal letters, job applications, letters overseas, and a variety of routine and tricky letters. Good, bad and middling examples are used to help beginners see for themselves the right and wrong ways of doing things. Ann Dobson is Principal of a secretarial training school with long experience of helping people improve their business skills.

183pp. illus. 1 85703 339 6. 2nd edition.

MAXIMISING YOUR MEMORY
How to train yourself to remember more

Peter Marshall

A powerful memory brings obvious advantages in educational, career and social terms. At school and college those certificates which provide a passport to a career depend heavily on what you can remember in the exam room. In the world of work, being able to recall details which slip the minds of colleagues will give you a competitive edge. In addition, one of the secrets of being popular with customers and friends is to remember their names and the little things which make them feel they matter to you. This book explains clearly how you can maximise your memory in order to achieve your academic, professional and personal goals. Peter Marshall is a member of the Applied Psychology Research Group of the University of London and works primarily on research into superior memory. He recently assisted with the production of Channel 4's Amazing Memory Show. He is also author of *How to Study and Learn* in this series.

128pp. illus. 1 85703 234 9.

WRITING A CV THAT WORKS
Developing and using your key marketing tool

Paul McGee

What makes a CV stand out from the crowd? How can you present yourself in the most successful way? This practical book shows you how to develop different versions of your CV for every situation. Reveal your hidden skills, identify your achievements and learn how to communicate these successfully. Different styles and uses for a CV are examined, as you discover the true importance of your most powerful marketing tool. Paul McGee is a freelance Trainer and Consultant for one of Britain's largest outplacement organisations. He conducts Marketing Workshops for people from all walks of life.

128pp. illus. 1 85703 365 5. 2nd edition.

MANAGING SUCCESSFUL TEAMS
How to achieve your objectives by working effectively with others

John Humphries

A team is a collection of individuals with their own ideas and abilities but with the willingness to share their ideas and use their abilities to achieve a common objective. It is generally recognised, therefore, that teams operate more effectively and efficiently than groups of individuals. This book is designed to help anyone who has the task of building and leading a team. It is full of sound, practical advice and contains a large selection of exercises that you can organise and run. John Humphries is a management trainer with over 20 years' experience of training people, both in the UK and abroad. He has written three other books in this series, including the very successful *Managing Through People*.

144pp. illus. 1 85703 282 9.